NAVIGATING LIFE AS A BROWN GIRL

FAHIMA ALI

AF006893

NAVIGATING LIFE AS A BROWN GIRL

A THERAPIST'S GUIDE FOR SOUTH ASIAN WOMEN

FAHIMA ALI

GREEN TREE
LONDON · OXFORD · NEW YORK · NEW DELHI · SYDNEY

GREEN TREE
Bloomsbury Publishing Plc
50 Bedford Square, London, WC1B 3DP, UK
Bloomsbury Publishing Ireland Limited
29 Earlsfort Terrace, Dublin 2, D02 AY28, Ireland

BLOOMSBURY, GREEN TREE and the Green Tree logo are trademarks of Bloomsbury Publishing Plc

First published in Great Britain 2026

Copyright © Fahima Ali, 2026

Fahima Ali has asserted her right under the Copyright, Designs and Patents Act, 1988, to be identified as Author of this work

For legal purposes the Acknowledgements on p. 220 constitute an extension of this copyright page

All rights reserved. No part of this publication may be: i) reproduced or transmitted in any form, electronic or mechanical, including photocopying, recording or by means of any information storage or retrieval system without prior permission in writing from the publishers; or ii) used or reproduced in any way for the training, development or operation of artificial intelligence (AI) technologies, including generative AI technologies. The rights holders expressly reserve this publication from the text and data mining exception as per Article 4(3) of the Digital Single Market Directive (EU) 2019/790

Bloomsbury Publishing Plc does not have any control over, or responsibility for, any third-party websites referred to or in this book. All internet addresses given in this book were correct at the time of going to press. The author and publisher regret any inconvenience caused if addresses have changed or sites have ceased to exist, but can accept no responsibility for any such changes

Disclaimer: The material contained in this book is for informational purposes only. No material in this publication is intended to be a substitute for professional medical advice, diagnosis or treatment. Always seek the advice of your GP or other qualified health care professional with any questions you may have regarding a medical condition, including mental health concerns, or treatment and before undertaking a new healthcare regime, and never disregard professional medical advice or delay in seeking it because of something you have read in this book

Please note that this book contains content that may be triggering for some. Specifically, it includes references to sexual abuse and domestic violence.

All case studies in this book are based on real experiences, but names and identifying details have been changed to protect the privacy of individuals.

A catalogue record for this book is available from the British Library

Library of Congress Cataloguing-in-Publication data has been applied for

ISBN: TPB: 978-1-3994-2019-8; eBook: 978-1-3994-2016-7

2 4 6 8 10 9 7 5 3 1

Typeset in Avenir Next LT Pro by Lumina Datamatics Ltd.
Printed and bound in Great Britain by Clays Ltd, Elcograf S.p.A.

To find out more about our authors and books visit www.bloomsbury.com and sign up for our newsletters
For product safety related questions contact productsafety@bloomsbury.com

To the women who came before me, and the ones still to come,
this book is yours.

To the ones who felt invisible in rooms they belonged in,
to those who questioned their worth because the world made them,
to the ones who held back tears to stay strong for everyone else,
I see you, I honour you, I'm walking beside you.

This is for the women who felt too much, not enough, or completely lost.
For the ones breaking cycles, finding themselves, speaking up, falling apart
and still choosing to begin again and again.

For those who are healing quietly, and those who are rising loudly, those being
courageous and breaking cycles, you are so deeply loved.

You are piecing yourselves back together, **peace by piece**.

And I'm so glad you're here.

From your fellow Brown girl,
Fahima

Contents

Introduction   8

1. The invisible life guide   20
2. Opening yourself up to the outside world   55
3. Marriage, in-laws, divorce and stigma   96
4. Who do you blame? Slowly breaking the cycle   141
5. Mental health   185

Conclusion   216
Resources   217
An invitation   219
Acknowledgements   220
Index   222

Introduction

For too long, you've been taught to be everything for everyone – except yourself. But now it's time to change the narrative.

Like so many Brown women, for years I carried around an invisible script, written for me long before I had a say, that told me how to be.

I grew up learning that my worth was measured by my ability to make others proud, to sacrifice quietly, to endure without complaint and to stay silent on topics that are taboo. But something always felt missing, like I was living a life that belonged to everyone else but me.

And there was a fire within me, a knowing, an urgency, that told me I was never meant to stay quiet. Silence was never my path.

So, I listened to that fire. I let it grow. I let it *free* me. I began to channel that voice, to let it shape the way I support, the way I speak, the way I connect, the way I work.

In doing so, I became the woman, the person and the therapist I was always meant to be: one who refuses to stay quiet, not just for myself but for every Brown woman who has ever been told to sit down, stay small or hold it all in.

And now, I am pouring every piece of that fire into this book. Because healing doesn't happen in silence. It happens when we dare to *speak*.

*****

In South Asian communities, we are taught that children are the legacy we leave behind, but legacies come in many forms. This book – these words, this truth – is mine. It holds my voice, my fight and my unshaken belief that change is possible. And if even one person finds themselves within these pages, if even one person feels seen, then every step, every struggle, every word will have meant something.

I am so grateful to finally have a space to be the voice of reason for the South Asian community – to be able to reach out to an audience that has been waiting to feel heard and understood for so long. It really is long overdue. My journey to becoming a therapist has brought many things to light, such as the lack of cultural understanding, lack of knowledge, lack of resources and lack of representation when it comes to the South Asian community.

I am Fahima, a Brown Bangladeshi British woman. I'm a daughter, a sister, a friend and an auntie. On social platforms, I'm known as @Fahima.Therapy, a 'Brown therapist' sharing experiences, breaking cycles, encouraging healthy relationships and bringing taboo topics to the surface.

A lot of you have connected with me through the content I put out on social media, and it's you who have inspired me to finally write a book. I know it's a struggle to navigate the system. I know there are many gaps and limited resources available for our community. I know some things take a lot of work. I know therapy can be expensive, and I know many people can't afford to be in therapy either at all or for very long.

Now, of course, this book isn't in itself therapy, but it is a guide so you don't feel so alone. Many of you reach out to me with questions, and one of the things that always stands out is the complexity the community faces that not everyone fully understands. So, I have written this book to give you some support.

The girl that was me

Many people think that, as a therapist, I must have it all figured out. That somehow my training, my profession, means I've found all the answers. But I want to be honest with you. I don't have it all figured out. I don't have all the answers. Before I became a therapist, I lived a life, though; so, alongside my professional experience, what I do have is lived experience and years of working on myself until I finally stepped into my power.

I know that life is rarely simple. It's messy, complicated and layered with both beauty and struggle, but in the middle of all that there's also the space to create something meaningful, something that speaks to you, something that nurtures your heart and your spirit.

As I look back at my own life, I can't help but think about the importance of connection. I talk about it often, and it's something we all crave. Growing up, I remember feeling like I had so many questions about myself, my culture and my place in the world, but I didn't always have the space to ask those questions or share those feelings. I wonder if you've ever felt the same way? You know, that longing for someone who'll listen without judgement, who'll just hear you out and let you speak freely. Children are naturally curious. They want to learn, they have so many questions and they ask 'why' all the time, but I was in a place where you just didn't ask.

I grew up with my family in East London, which has one of the largest populations of British Bangladeshis in the UK. From my early years to young adulthood, we moved many times, which meant I wasn't able to form solid relationships at school. It was a real struggle, as it meant that I never felt quite settled anywhere.

As a teen, my personal journey was disrupted by some self-hate for being Brown, a lot of questioning about my culture and my faith, and feelings of isolation; even though I was predominantly surrounded by other Brown kids, I didn't believe anyone else would be able to relate to me or the difficulties I had. Looking back, I'd like to say things felt normal, whatever that even means, but deep down I knew that what I felt wasn't right – and that at some point in my life, I would somehow need to deal with it.

I look back at that young girl, and she lived in a house that was always full at weekends, overflowing with guests, voices rising and falling, doors opening and closing, the scent of food filling the air. There was movement, noise, life. People laughed with ease, slipping into conversations as if it were the most natural thing in the world. She watched them – family, friends, guests – smiling, talking and existing in a way that seemed effortless.

She often wondered what it would feel like to truly be happy – to feel connected, to feel safe, to feel *anything* other than this constant sense of detachment. It was as if she were floating outside herself, watching her life unfold from a distance (what I would now, as a therapist, call 'depersonalisation'). The world around her felt unreal, like a hazy dream she couldn't quite touch or believe in (this is a classic description of 'derealisation'). Everything – people, places, emotions – felt far away, as though she were separated from them by an invisible barrier. She longed to feel grounded, to feel present, but she was stuck in this strange, distant space, yearning for something she couldn't quite reach.

She felt so lost, as if a part of her had come loose and drifted far away. If she'd been asked to describe it, she'd have told you it felt like standing on a train platform during rush hour: trains screaming past, their force pulling at her clothes, people rushing in and out, moving with urgency, with purpose. And her? She was just there: small, frozen, invisible. She wanted to move, to call out, to reach for someone, but her body wouldn't listen. And so, she just stood there, swallowed by the noise, by the world that never paused long enough to notice the girl who was too afraid to speak.

I look back at that young girl, who experienced endless sleepless nights and nightmares so severe she would wake up screaming. She was just a child, but what she carried was too heavy for her small body. She didn't know what it was, but as an adult I came to understand that she was struggling with complex post-traumatic stress disorder (CPTSD). Even writing these words makes me feel very vulnerable, though, because for a long time I didn't own it. As I revisit this now as an adult, I'm thinking, *How did she get here today?* But get here she did. And now you know why I speak about mental health.

Why I became a therapist

Mental health and connection are not just important to me; they are *everything*. I know what it's like to feel unseen, to move through life carrying pain that no one else seems to notice. I know what it's like to question your own emotions and to wonder whether what you're feeling is valid. This is why I do the work I do. It's why I create content to reach people who feel unheard and why I've written this book.

No one should have to go through their struggles alone, and you are not alone. Whatever you're carrying, whatever you've been through, I want you to know that I see you. I get it. And I hope, as you turn these pages, you derive even a small sense of comfort from knowing that someone out there understands – that healing, as painful and complicated as it will probably be, is possible.

Behind the content I share on social media, there's a woman who's been through her own struggles. I've had my fair share of hardships. I've felt confusion, I've questioned life and I've known the sting of isolation. I've confronted divorce, mental health struggles and the challenges that come from feeling misunderstood.

Then there's one struggle that many of us face in silence, something that's rarely spoken about in our community: sexual abuse. Was I believed? No. This is the first time I've revisited those experiences in so long, and it feels strange to put it out there into the world, but I know what it feels like to carry that shame, to feel like no one believes you or to have your experience dismissed. That kind of silence is so heavy, but I have put down a lot of weight from my younger years, weight that was never mine to carry; I am not a victim, and neither do I choose to call myself a survivor. I am Fahima.

That young girl was too young to understand why her body tensed up when certain footsteps approached, but she learned quickly that silence kept her safe and that swallowing the pain was easier than speaking it. She also learned quickly that no one would believe her, because little girls like her - girls who were raised to be obedient, to respect their elders, to never question - were expected to endure, not to fight.

She tried to convince herself it wasn't real. Maybe she imagined it. Maybe she was wrong. Maybe *she* was the problem. Because when the secret did accidentally come out, it was met with disbelief. *How dare you? How shameful.* And just like that, the door to safety slammed shut. The shame clung to her like a second skin, whispering that she was dirty, that if people knew, they would look at her differently. She was young, but she carried the burden of someone else's sins. She smiled when she was supposed to and laughed when it was expected, playing the part so well that no one ever saw the cracks.

And yet, in the quiet of her room, when she stared up at the ceiling and tried to push the memories away, the betrayal cut deep. Something inside her burned: a small voice, buried under layers of shame and fear. *The only way to survive is to play the game everyone else plays: keeping up appearances.* Because when the world refuses to see your pain, you start to wonder if it was ever real to begin with. As an adult I'd hear, 'It's not your fault', but that young girl always knew it wasn't; she just didn't understand *why*.

She played the game of life well. Among her friends, she was known for her infectious laughter, the kind that drew people in and made friendships seem effortless. Connecting with others came naturally to her, or so it seemed, but was she truly building genuine bonds or was she simply pouring herself into others so she didn't need to look within?

Over time, I've let go of many people. The more I've worked on myself, the more I've tuned into who I truly am and the spaces and people

I want around me. Now, as an adult, while I still have the ability to connect deeply, my circle has grown smaller, more intentional, more meaningful.

The importance of support

I'm the middle child of eight and, as you can imagine, it was difficult for my mother to give us all individual attention, particularly given the other roles she had to play. That meant, to a large extent, I grew up feeling isolated and alone. I had to teach myself about the world based on observations about my environment and overheard conversations, and I didn't necessarily feel that I could always rely on my parents to be there for me.

When I think about my divorce, what stands out most isn't the process itself but the one thing that made it easier: support. Divorce was confusing, but I felt liberated making the choice – a choice I didn't know I had – and the support I received made all the difference. I still remember overhearing my father on the phone, his words cutting through the chaos: 'I don't care how many times my daughter has to go through divorce; she is like gold.' In that moment, his support was like a shield, giving me courage and softening the blows and judgements I thought I'd face from the community.

I was surprised, because the community that I grew up in looked down on divorce, and I'd already mentally prepared what I'd say to them if my parents told me to 'go back'. I was ready to break the cycle, but I saw my parents breaking it, too. Of course, they were sad and they wanted more for me, because marriage for them was a big deal, but I applaud them for not caring about what other people thought.

I share this because so many women endure divorce in isolation, burdened not just by the loss of a marriage but by the absence of support, and for many that absence of support becomes the deepest wound of all. I know you may feel caught between the desire to meet those external expectations and the need to honour who you are inside. This is a common struggle in our community, and it does feel isolating, but I see you and I understand the weight of trying to balance it all.

People often say to me, 'Fahima, how do you do it? As a therapist, how do you listen to people's pain every day? Doesn't it ever feel too much?' Honestly, no. It never feels too much. Because this work isn't just something I do; it's something I *am*. I hold space for people who are suffering not because I have to, but because I *can*. Because I know what it means to feel unseen, unheard and alone. I know what it's like to feel lost and to need holding. And if I can be the person who listens, who validates, who can gently get someone to see parts of themselves they haven't seen before to give them courage, then I am doing exactly what I was meant to do. I see it as my purpose.

Every person who walks through my door is carrying a story – one they may have never spoken aloud before. And the fact that they choose to share it with me? That they allow me into their most vulnerable moments? That trust is something I will never take for granted. It is a privilege and an honour.

I don't see this work as absorbing pain; I see it as witnessing resilience. I get to sit with people as they expose their deepest wounds, and I also get to see them find strength they didn't know they had. I watch them reclaim themselves, step by step, and that, more than anything, is why I love what I do. Because healing is not about fixing; it's about holding, understanding and walking alongside someone as they find their way back to themselves.

My hope is that, through this book, you will understand that you don't have to go through it alone – that you can share your thoughts and emotions freely, without fear of being misunderstood or judged. This is a space where you can truly be yourself, a space where we can navigate these experiences together, one step at a time.

Being Brown

As a society, we often fail to acknowledge and understand that people from different cultural backgrounds experience different lived-in circumstances, which in turn shape and impact their mental health in distinctive ways. The solution isn't one-size-fits-all – a concept that can be damaging for people's mental health, especially for people of colour.

During my training to become a therapist, I had to complete an exercise that asked me to choose my race, but I couldn't tick any of the options; no box read 'South Asian'. I looked up at my tutor and said, 'None of these are mine.' She replied, 'Just pick the closest one.' I have never forgotten that moment. How could I pick a race that wasn't me? I felt invisible and unheard. But afterwards, I realised that the point of this exercise had specifically been to generate the feelings that are raised when you are forced to be something you are not. I already knew those emotions, because that is how the Brown community generally feels, but the aim of the exercise made sense.

Becoming a therapist was never just a career path for me; it was a journey of breaking and rebuilding, of questioning everything I thought I knew about myself. It felt like I had to take myself apart, piece by piece, examining every fragment of who I was, sitting with the discomfort of not fully understanding myself, and then slowly, carefully, putting it all back together so that it made sense.

I had to learn to build a relationship with every part of me, including the parts I'd ignored, the parts I'd been ashamed of and even the parts shaped by pain. I learned to love them. When I was young, I used to blame the culture, the traditions, the system or the faith, and part of the work I've done was to separate the people who brought me pain from the culture, the traditions, the system and the faith. It was never about any of those things, and if it was, it meant I disliked who I am. It took time, and only in my 30s did I finally feel like I was connecting with myself and had reclaimed myself, wholly and unapologetically.

I don't want people to judge my culture or my faith, because they are important to me, and I haven't always felt that other therapists and those in the mental health industry understand my experiences. This lack of cultural knowledge and awareness really became obvious when I started to create content on social media. I was blown away by the positive messages and comments I received, and it made me realise how many people felt the way I did.

Thousands of people who came across my page mentioned how relieved they were to finally see a Brown therapist exist, someone who understood them, so they didn't need to spend their therapy sessions trying to explain their culture; and these were just through seeing videos they resonated with. It confirmed that many of you are suffering in silence, not knowing that what we are experiencing is more than valid, and it was both overwhelming and heartbreaking.

Brown communities face some specific challenges, including immigration, intergenerational conflicts and discrimination, but, most discouragingly, the stigma around mental health in our community is still huge. There is deep and ingrained shame around talking about psychological struggles, and not everyone can speak freely and openly about mental health. I receive messages on a daily basis from people who don't know whether what they are experiencing is 'severe enough' to get support, let alone where they should go to get the support, which is where this book comes in.

How this book aims to help

Cultural context is so important. I'm going to look at issues based around the different stages of life that you navigate as a Brown girl, including family dynamics, identity, how you engage with the outside world, marriage and divorce. But before we begin, I want to stress that not everything I write will be the experience of all Brown girls reading this. Everyone's experience is unique. There may be parts that resonate with some of you and parts that won't, but I hope it will help you explore the nuances and complexities of our culture.

For each topic I discuss, I'll outline the traditions (i.e., the 'traditional narrative'), and then I'll look at how we can begin to dismantle those traditions. I'll also give you some practical exercises to encourage self-reflection as you begin to work through this. Of course, some families are more traditional than others, and there may be several different traditions running within a family, but my hope is that this book will help you explore who you are and who you want to be.

This book is for the Brown woman who has carried more than she should. For the one who has learned to put herself last, to silence her needs, to shrink parts of herself just to be accepted. For the one who constantly manages that dual identity, living between the traditions and values of the country her parents came from and the country where she lives now. For the one who feels trapped between those cultural expectations and her own desires, and who wonders if she's asking for too much just by wanting to exist freely.

If you struggle with parts of yourself, this book is for you. If you find yourself saying, 'I hate being Brown', this book is for you. If you question your worth as a woman, this book is for you. If you feel confused about what your purpose is, this book is for you. If you are sick of being told how to live, this book is for you. If you are trapped between who you are and who you are expected to be, this book is for you. If you are told to be grateful and feel guilty for wanting more, this book is for you.

It's also important you understand that this book is not here to judge you. It's not here to tell you who you should be. It's here to hold you, to create space for the parts of you that have been neglected, dismissed or misunderstood. It's a book about all the things we don't talk about enough: the deep, raw and painful realities of being a South Asian woman.

We'll talk about family dynamics: the invisible expectations, the weight of being a good daughter and the silent sacrifices so many of us make. We'll talk about how 'What will people say?' is not just a phrase but a tool of control, one that's shaped our decisions and kept us bound in fear. We'll explore marriage not as a fairy tale or a duty but as a reality filled with complexity, cultural pressure and, sometimes, heartbreak. We'll talk about divorce – the shame, the stigma and the way so many women hang on in pain just to avoid the divorce label. We'll sit with the reality of mental health struggles, the loneliness of suffering in silence, the hesitation to seek therapy and the way in which mental health is often brushed aside in our homes as if it doesn't exist.

But this book isn't just about pain. It's about recognition and healing. It's about giving voice to the experiences that have weighed you down and offering tools to help you navigate them. You'll find reflections, guidance and case studies of women who have walked similar paths – women who have struggled, questioned and ultimately found ways to reclaim parts of themselves. As you read, I don't want you to feel rushed or pushed or that you're being told what to do. I want you to feel understood, like you have a companion within these pages – someone who's walked through similar struggles, who sees the layers of pain and complexity and who's gently encouraging you to see yourself with more compassion.

No matter where you are on your journey, whether you're questioning, healing, resisting or just beginning to unravel the weight of your past and present, this book is for you. And I hope that as you turn the pages, you find not just understanding but also a quiet, steady belief that you are worthy of more. More love, more gentleness, more space to exist in a way that feels true to you.

I know from my own experience that there's something incredibly powerful about doing the work, even when it feels impossible, but healing doesn't happen overnight. It's not a single moment of clarity, a perfect step-by-step process or a destination where everything suddenly makes sense. It's slow. It's messy. Some days, it will feel like you're unravelling more than you're rebuilding. Some days, it will feel like nothing has changed. But in time, you'll begin to see the shifts, the moments where you speak up when you would have once stayed silent, where you give yourself permission to rest without guilt, where you trust yourself a little more than you did before. And those moments? They are everything.

It took me years to do this work. But the moment you start doing the work, the moment you begin to like who you are, to feel peace settle into your bones, to move through the world with a contentment, you'll notice something. Others will notice it too – and not everyone will like your growth.

Some will be uncomfortable with the change they see in you. They've built an image of you based on your struggles, your suffering, your lowest moments. Whether consciously or unconsciously, they expect you to stay there. But you'll notice it, because by then you'll have learned discernment. They expect you to wear your wounds like a permanent marker of what you've been through, and when you don't – when you dare to heal, to rise, to look *radiant* despite what you've endured – it unsettles them: *How is she okay? How does she look so good after everything she's been through? How does she do it? She must be faking it.* Healing disrupts the narrative, and your happiness forces them to confront their own stagnation. Your growth is proof that transformation is possible, but only for those who choose it. And not everyone is ready to do so.

Hear me when I say this: you do not owe anyone your suffering. You do not have to shrink back into who you used to be just to make others comfortable. Growth will expose the ones who only knew how to love the old version of you, but there will also be the ones who celebrate you, the ones who see your light and who feel inspired not threatened by it, the ones who clap for you, who feel joy simply because you are finally at peace. Hold on to them. Those are your people.

As you read this book, I hope you feel a sense of community, of shared experience, of knowing that your pain is real and valid – that there are others who have felt what you feel, who have struggled in the same way and who are walking alongside you in their own process of healing. Look out for this symbol ⌘ for exercises you can do to reflect on your own journey.

Take your time. Pause when you need to. Reflect. Come back to these pages whenever you need to feel seen, whenever you need a reminder that your journey, your pain, your healing, your growth matters. And if nothing else, let this be an invitation to start, to take up space, to allow yourself to exist fully, beyond the expectations, beyond the fear, beyond what has been handed down to you. You deserve that, and I will be here, holding this space for you, every step of the way.

Your fellow Brown girl…

> ### Before we begin
>
> I want to acknowledge that there are many topics that I have not been able to touch on due to space limitations. If you do not see your specific circumstance discussed, then please know that your experience is valid and that I see you.

1. The invisible life guide

You've probably spent much of your life watching and silently absorbing the world around you. As a Brown child, you saw your elders moving through their lives with what seemed like certainty. They didn't explain their choices and you weren't invited to question them. Instead, you were expected to follow, to nod and agree, to obey without hesitation – because that was the way things were. You watched, and you absorbed the lesson: *This is what it means to be a woman.*

Why can't you stay over at a friend's house? *Because you can't*. Why must you prioritise family duty over personal ambition? *Because that's just how it is*. Why are life decisions – what to study, when to marry, whom to marry – often made on your behalf? *Because your elders know best*. These aren't just South Asian family traditions; they're deeply ingrained expectations passed down as unquestionable truths, and they form what I call the 'invisible life guide': a set of rules that dictate how you should move through the world as a Brown woman. They tell you how to dress, speak, behave and even feel. Breaking them will bring disappointment or shame, but they are unspoken.

The Traditional Narrative

No one explicitly explains it to you, but the invisible life guide shapes how you live your life. It tells you what's expected of you as a woman, as a daughter and as a member of a family or a community, especially in a South Asian context. It's not something you consciously choose to follow; it's something you internalise, because that's just *how things are done*.

Our understanding of the invisible life guide starts early, usually in childhood. Maybe no one sits you down to teach you those rules, but you learn them by watching. You see how your mother sacrifices her time and energy for the family, how your father makes decisions without consulting anyone else, how girls are praised for being obedient, quiet and helpful. These rules are not written down and no one talks about them out loud, but the messages are clear:

- This is how you should behave.
- This is what's expected of you.
- This is what success looks like.

The invisible life guide tells you to:

- do well in school;
- help out at home without complaining;
- get married at the 'right' age;
- have children and prioritise your family;
- be a good daughter, wife, mother and community member;
- avoid jeopardising your family's honour with your actions and choices;
- never act without considering what other people will say.

Following the guide means following a path that's rooted in traditions and social norms and that influences your unconscious choices, because it's so deeply ingrained in the culture around you. In truth, neither your parents nor their parents made the rules, and those who came before you were following the invisible life guide, too, but these unspoken rules are still rigidly in place, even when the world around them has changed. However, it's worth noting that these rules can sometimes change and shift as families move to new countries or confront new realities. Let's explore the impact of this invisible life guide further.

Controlling behaviour

'What do you want? What makes you happy? What would you like for yourself?' When was the last time anyone asked you these questions? If they make you feel uncomfortable, it may be because you've been conditioned to prioritise others over yourself. Or perhaps when you did share your hopes or dreams, you were met with indifference, leaving you feeling that your emotions and desires were unimportant.

Think back to when you were told to *'be a good girl'*. It seems such an innocent phrase, yet in Brown families it's loaded with expectations. You were taught early on that being good meant being quiet, being agreeable, not challenging authority and definitely not questioning the rules. *'Don't talk back',* they'd say, as if speaking your truth was essentially wrong. Gradually, you stopped just hearing these words; you began to feel them. You watched. You observed. You noticed what brought praise and what brought disapproval, and you internalised it all. You noticed how your siblings or other children were praised for achievements that aligned with what the family valued: obedience, academic success or silence in moments when they should have spoken up. You noticed the unspoken judgement when someone chose something different.

You might not have realised it then, but those moments in your childhood, those subtle messages of control, shaped you. A glance, a stare, when you did or said something they didn't like was enough to tell you that they disapproved – that you had somehow failed. And that stare? It carried so much more than words ever could. It wasn't just disapproval; it felt like rejection. It felt like you were being told you weren't good enough, that you were betraying the very people who raised you. As a result, you found yourself conforming to others' expectations, even though at the same time you may have felt disconnected from your own needs and desires.

Maternal role models

You probably grew up watching your mother tirelessly looking after everyone in the family. She probably did the cooking, the cleaning, the endless little things that made the house run smoothly, while your dad went off to work. And you probably saw your mother praised for the sacrifices she made, for the way she let go of her own dreams to serve others. You saw how the approval she received was tied to her ability to stay silent, to avoid conflict, to put everyone else's needs ahead of her own, and that message bled into you quietly and powerfully.

In fact, you probably saw it time and time again: Brown women being praised not because they thrived but because they endured. You saw how the community almost celebrated their ability to carry pain, to struggle in silence, to shoulder unimaginable burdens without breaking. It was as if their worth was directly tied to how much they could tolerate, how much they could sacrifice and how little they demanded in return.

The more they could handle, the more respect they received. And you watched, taking in every moment, internalising every silent message.

Think back to those moments growing up. Did you ever notice how much of life seemed like a performance? Your parents might have played their roles flawlessly, providing, working and keeping the house running, but was something missing? Perhaps warmth, laughter, an emotional connection between them? My guess is they were simply doing what they had been taught to do: fulfil their responsibilities and keep going, no matter what, because that's what the invisible life guide tells you to do.

But who did your mother turn to when her emotions overwhelmed her? Did you see her confide in anyone when she was sad, frustrated or angry? Bound by secrecy and the fear of judgement, perhaps she couldn't let her emotions go beyond the four walls of the home, so maybe she turned to her children instead, leaning on you in ways you may not have fully understood at the time.

Or maybe she didn't express anything at all. You saw her smile through pain and bury her feelings deep within her, because showing them would have been a sign of weakness. You might have even heard her say things like, *'It's just how life is'* or *'This is what we do for family'*. You believed her, because at the time it made sense, but there was also something heartbreaking in the way she lived.

You might recall how she looked at you sometimes, her eyes heavy, her expression distant, as if she wanted to say something but couldn't. Maybe you caught glimpses of her sadness in the moments when no one else was around. Or perhaps you noticed how quickly she dismissed her own needs, telling you, *'I'm fine'*, even when you could see she wasn't.

For many Brown women, these scenarios will feel all too familiar. Our mothers' identities were often tied entirely to what they *did* for others, not how they felt. Their value was measured in the meals they cooked, the sacrifices they made and their ability not to show emotion, because the invisible life guide teaches you not with words but with actions, with silence, with sacrifice.

Endurance test

Strength has often been represented by the endurance of the woman who stays in her marriage no matter how unhappy she is. Even in situations where her emotional well-being is in shreds, society perceives her as 'strong' for holding everything together. Sometimes, the bar is set heartbreakingly low, with people saying, *'At least he doesn't hit her'*, as if that is enough to justify the absence of love or respect. And when she stays, despite the pain, she is applauded for her strength, as if her suffering is proof of her character.

Do you define the word *strength* by what you saw and absorbed growing up? By the sacrifices your mother made, putting everyone else's needs before her own, swallowing her exhaustion, attending to guests with a smile, even when all she wanted was to rest? By the way she saved the best food for others or how she never bought anything for herself? Or maybe by the way she tolerated disrespect from in-laws or family members, because keeping the peace mattered more than her own dignity?

As you grew up yourself, you sought approval, validation and acceptance in the same way. Crying would have been seen as weakness, and showing too much emotion made others uncomfortable, so to show how strong you were, you probably suppressed your own emotions and learned to hold them in, to put on a brave face, to harden yourself against the world. You started to think that being strong wasn't about living authentically or pursuing happiness; it was about how much suffering you could put up with. You thought, *If I can just endure more, if I can just keep going, they will see me and they will finally value me.*

So, you tried to embody their definition of strength. You poured yourself into being everything they wanted. You became the daughter who never spoke back, the sister who always gave in, the wife who sacrificed her needs, the mother who never put herself first. You excelled in school, hoping your achievements would earn their pride. You dressed to meet with their approval, spoke in the way they deemed respectable and made choices that prioritised their comfort over your own. But no matter how much you endured, how much you sacrificed or how many times you were the 'good girl', it never seemed enough. The approval felt short-lived and the validation was superficial.

And what about the cost of that kind of strength? What about the parts of yourself you had to abandon to keep up the image of being strong? The strength the invisible life guide teaches you leaves no room for vulnerability, no space for softness, but real strength is so much more than sacrificing, suppressing and enduring.

Failing to follow the guide

According to the invisible life guide, the achievements that should be celebrated are the milestones that make everyone smile with pride: the marriages that happen at the 'right' time, the children who excel in school, the families who maintain their harmonious image. In South Asian communities, these are the people who are placed on pedestals and applauded. But what about the others? The ones who carry complexity, pain or choices that challenge tradition? There is no plan for those whose lives don't fit the mould and who don't follow the guide.

There's the auntie who left her marriage, her name often spoken in hushed tones, if at all. The cousin who struggled in school and faded from conversations, as though academic success is the only measure of worth. Or the family that seems to be unravelling under the weight of their struggles, becoming invisible in a community that demands perfection. But they didn't disappear; they were intentionally pushed aside, hidden like secrets that didn't belong in the carefully curated narrative of success. They were labelled failures or rebels, not for whom they truly were but to keep the illusion of perfection intact.

What if you were taught that your husband would take care of you, but he can't, whether financially, emotionally or physically? What if, over time, you realise that you're not emotionally connected to him and the relationship feels hollow? What if you find out he is unfaithful or abusive? What do you do when the life you were shown doesn't fit into the reality you're living?

What happens if you're a single mum, raising your children on your own, without the support network you were led to believe you'd always have? Your invisible life guide never mentioned that reality. You weren't shown what it looks like to manage the finances on your own, to balance work, home and self-care while trying to maintain some aspect of peace.

When things don't go according to plan, when relationships don't work out, when careers don't fulfil you or when traditions clash with your personal values, you're left feeling lost. Your invisible life guide doesn't offer solutions for the moments when life takes an unexpected turn. It tells you to make it work, no matter what.

Brown women are taught this, often without words, but what happens to those who don't follow the invisible guidelines? They're the ones whose names are spoken with a sigh, a shake of the head, a quiet warning wrapped in pity: *'Look at her; what a shame.'* They are not celebrated. They are tolerated at best, avoided at worst. They become the cautionary tales, the examples of what *not* to be.

You are taught that ignoring the guide means isolation; that you will be the one who is ignored at family gatherings, whose choices are met with forced smiles and silent judgements: *She's lost her way.* And so, you learn to stay in line. Not always because you want to, but because the alternative of being unseen, unwelcome and unloved feels too heavy to bear. But here's what I want you to hear: you don't have to live your life on autopilot. You don't have to follow a path simply because it's what others expect of you.

Whether you choose to follow the invisible life guide or not is up to you, yet one thing I'd encourage you to do is give yourself permission to stop and ask yourself questions, even hard ones: *Why is this important? Does this fit the life I want for myself? Maybe I can have more than one plan for myself?* When you ask these questions, you open the door to understanding. You give yourself the power to make choices that feel right for you, not because they've been handed down but because they align with who you truly are. And if the answers don't make sense, or the traditions don't fit any more, you have the power to create your own answers and your own traditions. That's where the next section of this chapter comes in.

Dismantling The Traditional Narrative

It's now time to pause and unpick, and to ask some perhaps difficult questions. Here, we will begin the work of dismantling the narratives of the invisible life guide, gently but firmly. I will walk you through this process, helping you to examine your emotions and recognise where these beliefs come from, why they hold such power and, most importantly, how you can start unlearning them.

This is not about blame but about choice. It's about seeing yourself clearly, not through the lens of duty or sacrifice but through your own eyes. Doing this work requires you to face the painful truths of your upbringing, to unlearn the lessons you've carried for so long and to make choices that may feel foreign or even wrong at first; however, other people's sacrifices don't have to define you, and their struggles don't have to be yours.

The invisible life guide is not written in stone and it can be changed. The first step to reclaiming your life is recognising that the guide exists and that it can affect your life. Once you see it for what it is – a set of unspoken norms – you can begin to question it by asking yourself the following questions:

- Does the invisible life guide align with the life I want to live?
- Does it prepare me for when things don't turn out that way?
- Does it build my strength and resilience?
- Are there parts of it I want to keep and honour?
- Are there parts of it I want to let go of?

As I say, this isn't about disrespecting or rejecting your family. It's about finding a balance between honouring where you come from and creating a life that feels authentic to you. It's about learning what to do when the invisible life guide fails you or when you want something it doesn't offer. You deserve to live a life that feels whole, even if that means rewriting the rules along the way. You have the right to ask questions, to seek clarity and to take the path that makes sense for *you*.

Acknowledging the invisible life guide doesn't mean abandoning your culture or your roots. It means making space to understand it, challenge it and adapt it to fit your life. It means giving yourself permission to live with intention rather than obligation. It means allowing fluidity in place of rigidity. This is your journey, but you don't need to make it alone. Let me walk alongside you, offering you the compassion, validation and guidance you may not even realise you crave. Together, we can rewrite the guide. Let's explore how with the help of some exercises along the way.

Passing it on

Over time, you have internalised the voices of expectation that tell you to be obedient and selfless, and now, even when no one else is pressuring you, their thoughts and choices have become your thoughts and choices. This is how the cycle continues, quietly yet powerfully, shaping how you move through your daily life, but the cycle can be broken if you open yourself up to different possibilities and make space to think about the 'what ifs'. If you don't do this, you are allowing yourself to remain trapped in the same patterns that have shaped your life for years.

You are the perfect daughter who never questions, the mother who gives endlessly and the wife who sacrifices without complaint. You avoid confrontation at all costs, telling yourself it's to keep the peace, but inside your heart it feels like chaos. In your inner world, unspoken emotions and unmet needs clash, and the war rages between what you want and what you've been taught is acceptable.

You put others' needs above your own, not because you don't matter but because that's what's always been expected of you. The moment you consider prioritising yourself, whether it's by pursuing your career, taking time for your hobbies or even just saying 'no', a wave of guilt crashes over you. That guilt states that you're failing as a South Asian daughter, mother or wife, even though deep down you know that isn't true. But guilt is persistent and keeps you chained to the same expectations that are suffocating you.

And then there's the deeper struggle, the one that's harder to name. It's the suppression of *you*. The parts of you that crave discovery, exploration and individuality remain hidden, because you've learned that being too much *you* might upset the balance. You want to honour tradition, to stay rooted in the values you were raised with, but you also feel the pull to dismantle what no longer serves you.

This tension, between holding on and letting go, leaves you feeling stuck, as though stepping too far in either direction might make you lose a part of yourself or risk disappointing those you care about. This is the pain of living in a world that asks you to give everything and then, when you've given all you have, asks for even more – and it's a deeply personal wound that many South Asian women carry.

The 'Inheritance reflection' exercise below will help you understand how this wound manifested for your ancestors – and what it means to begin healing.

Exercise: Inheritance reflection

Like you, did your mother wait for someone to see her, to acknowledge all that she gave, to tell her she was enough? And did she learn to live with the emptiness, carrying it silently, never questioning it, because she believed this was just the way life had to be? This exercise helps you contemplate the cycle that you need to break.

Imagine sitting across from the women who came before you: your mother, your grandmother and the generations before them. Picture them in their younger years, before they were shaped by expectation and duty.

Now ask yourself these questions:

- *What dreams did they have before they were told they couldn't dream?*
- *What parts of themselves did they suppress to fit into the roles they were expected to fill?*
- *If they had been given the choice to honour their true selves, what might their lives have looked like?*
- *What would they say if they saw you now, standing at the edge of breaking free?*

Sit with this for a moment. Let their unheard stories settle in you. Then ask yourself two further questions:

- *If you continue on the same path, what will the next generation of women inherit from you?*
- *If you choose differently, what new story can you create for the next generation?*

You are not just challenging norms for yourself; you are healing something much deeper. You are giving future South Asian daughters, nieces and younger sisters permission to live fully. Your courage to break the cycle is a gift they will one day thank you for.

The cost of invisibility

One of the most important truths I want you to recognise is that living by the invisible life guide comes at a cost – a cost so heavy, so deep-seated, that you might not have acknowledged it even to yourself.

You've been carrying a weight, a painful, emotional burden, because when you live according to these unwritten and unspoken standards, you find yourself in a constant state of self-doubt. That voice in your mind never truly goes away: *Am I good enough? Will*

I ever be good enough? You measure every step you take, every word you say, by the invisible rules, and with that comes an overwhelming fear of failure: the fear that if you misstep, if you pause and maybe, just maybe, say 'no', you won't just disappoint yourself; you'll disappoint everyone around you.

The 'Two circles' exercise below will allow you to start to appreciate the weight of guilt in your life.

Exercise: Two circles

Guilt can be all-consuming. It creeps into every corner of your life, telling you that if you even think about prioritising your own desires and your own dreams, you're being selfish. And so, you silence those desires. You tell yourself they don't matter – that your dreams can wait. But how long can they wait? Days turn into years, and soon you realise that you've built a life that revolves around everyone else with no room for yourself.

This exercise is designed to help you see how the person you are, and the actions you take, are shaped by guilt. But more importantly, it shows you the person who might start to emerge if you were less weighed down, less distorted, by that guilt:

1. Take a blank sheet of paper and draw two circles on it.
2. In the first circle, write down everything you do for others, your responsibilities, the roles you fulfil, the acts of care and the ways in which you make others comfortable. This could include cooking, being emotionally available, following family expectations or choosing a career that pleases others.
3. In the second circle, write down everything you would do if guilt wasn't stopping you. Think about the passions you've buried, the adventures you'd like to have, things you'd say no to and the decisions you would make if you weren't afraid of disappointing others. This could be as simple as taking a solo trip, pursuing a creative hobby, setting boundaries or making a decision based on what feels right for *you*.
4. Now, take a step back and look at both circles. Which one feels more like *you*? What small step can you take today to honour even a piece of that second circle?

Holding back

When you start to recognise the flaws in the traditional narrative, the invisible life guide that has been passed down through generations and continues to be perpetuated, you begin to see how incomplete and even damaging it really is.

It teaches you how to be obedient but not how to set boundaries. It emphasises respect for elders but never teaches them to respect you in return. You're told that marriage is the ultimate goal but are never taught how to navigate healthy relationships, recognise red flags or advocate for your needs.

Emotional suppression is encouraged in the name of family harmony, but you're not taught how to process difficult feelings, communicate effectively or manage conflict without guilt. You're expected to be selfless and accommodating, yet no one prepares you for the resentment and burnout that come from constantly putting others before yourself.

Financial independence isn't emphasised, especially for women, leaving many feeling trapped in unhealthy dynamics with no escape plan. The result? A generation of women who feel lost, overwhelmed and unprepared for the very life to which they were told to aspire. The assumption is that life will unfold in a very predictable, orderly way, and that if you just follow the right steps by being a good girl, graduating, getting married and having children, everything will fall into place. If you're a good girl, the assumption is that you should just *know*, but that's not how life works.

The guide hasn't prepared you for the real world. It hasn't given you the tools to navigate the complexities and challenges that you face now as an adult. It hasn't taught you how to build a life where you feel secure in yourself, how to make decisions for your happiness or how to manage your emotions in a healthy way. And you're being held back by what you haven't been taught and by what you've been wrongly taught.

You can use the 'Self-limiting beliefs' exercise below to identify the things you've internalised that are holding you back.

Exercise: Self-limiting beliefs

I'm willing to guess that there have been times when you've felt helpless and trapped. You've probably questioned your ability to make your own decisions, to assert yourself. The invisible life guide teaches you to look outward for validation and approval rather than inward to recognise your own power and potential, and it makes you believe you have no options, but that really isn't the case.

The invisible life guide teaches you to move through life using rules that often hold you back. You may not even realise how deeply these beliefs are limiting you. This exercise will help you uncover, challenge and rewrite the messages that keep you stuck:

1. **Identifying your self-limiting beliefs**
   - Grab a journal and write down your honest answers to these questions:
     - What is one area of life where I feel stuck or unfulfilled? (e.g. relationships, career, self-worth, setting boundaries, emotional expression)
     - What belief do I hold that keeps me from changing this situation? *(e.g. I can't disappoint my parents; If I set boundaries, I will lose people; Marriage is my ultimate purpose; Speaking up makes me a bad daughter)*
     - Where did I learn this belief? (Was it from family, culture, past experiences? When was the first time I remember hearing it?)

2. **Examining the cost of this limiting belief**
   - How has this belief impacted my choices and well-being?
   - What opportunities have I missed because I accepted this as truth?
   - How does this belief make me feel about myself? (e.g. small, powerless, anxious, guilty, resentful)
   - For example, your responses could look something like this:
     - Belief: If I seek therapy, people will think I'm weak.
     - Impact: I avoid getting help even when I feel overwhelmed. I suffer in silence and feel isolated.
     - Opportunities: I could have learned tools to heal, but I let stigma stop me.
     - Emotion: I feel stuck, anxious and unsupported.

3. **Challenging the limiting belief**
   - Now, let's challenge the belief by questioning its validity:
     - Is this belief objectively true, or is it something I was conditioned to believe?

- Do I know people who have broken this belief and thrived?
- What would I tell a friend who was struggling with this belief?

4. **Rewriting the narrative**
   - Rewrite your limiting belief into an empowering belief.
   - Say it out loud or write it on a Post-it note where you'll see it daily.
   - For example, you could rewrite your limiting belief like this:
     - Limiting belief: A good daughter sacrifices everything.
     - Empowering belief: A good daughter is also allowed to have her own life.

5. **Taking one small action**
   - Now that you've reframed your belief, commit to taking one small step to reinforce it. For example:
     - If your belief was about seeking help, research one therapist or mental health resource.
     - If your belief was about self-worth, do something just for yourself, with/without guilt.

The beliefs passed down to you were not facts; they were fears. You get to build your resilience and your skills. *Let that land*.

Brown girl guilt

Guilt is a recurring theme throughout this book, because it is something that so many of you are deeply familiar with, especially as South Asian women. It's an emotion that has been modelled for you in countless ways, often without you or the person doing the modelling even realising it.

From the moment you were born, guilt was tied to obedience. It was intertwined with your very being, subtly associating compliance, sacrifice and putting others first with guilt. This became so ingrained in you that it was almost automatic. You didn't need to be told; you just felt it. The moment you considered putting yourself first, guilt would rise, reminding you of what you 'should' be doing.

But what I want you to understand is this: guilt, like any other emotion, comes and goes. It's a feeling that enters your body, just like sadness, joy or anger. It rises within you, often overwhelming you, and then dissolves. It is not permanent. What happens, though, is that guilt starts to *control* you.

It starts to dictate your actions. You obey it, just as you've been taught to obey other external expectations, and guilt becomes the voice telling you to sacrifice, to please, to prioritise everyone else's needs over your own.

Of course, you feel guilty when you try to step into new spaces, spaces that are unfamiliar and unexplored by those who came before you. It's natural to feel guilty when you're venturing into territory where no one has supported you, or when those who dared to do so in the past were rejected, judged or even disowned by the community. It's terrifying to face the possibility of being cast aside, of standing alone. But that guilt, painful as it feels, doesn't define you.

Let's use the 'Healthy and unhealthy guilt' exercise below to explore the different types of guilt you may feel.

Exercise: Healthy and unhealthy guilt

You've been conditioned to believe that guilt means you're doing something wrong, that it's a sign of disrespect or rebellion. But guilt is just an emotion – it doesn't carry inherent truth. It's not telling you that you're a bad person. It's simply a reflection of your fear, your hesitation and your uncertainty as you try to create a life that aligns with your own truth rather than the invisible life guide.

When guilt rises, it's important to notice it without letting it control you. Instead of surrendering to its pressure, take a moment to pause and acknowledge that this is a feeling, not a commandment. You're allowed to feel guilty, but you're not required to act on that feeling. You're allowed to shape your own path, even if it feels difficult and uncomfortable. This exercise will help you begin to do that:

1. **Identify the guilt you're feeling**
    - Take a moment to reflect. What is making you feel guilty right now?
    - Is it something you did or didn't do? (e.g. saying 'no' to a family event, making a decision they disapprove of, prioritising your needs over cultural expectations)
    - Who is making you feel guilty? (e.g. your parents, your community, yourself)
    - What is the underlying message behind this guilt? (*I'm selfish; I'm not a good daughter; I should be more grateful*)

2. **Is this guilt healthy or conditioned?**
Ask yourself the following questions to determine if this guilt is justified or imposed.
   - Healthy guilt (comes from your values):
     - *Did I actually harm someone, and do I need to make amends?*
     - *Does this guilt align with my personal morals and integrity?*
     - *Will taking responsibility help me grow as a person?*
   - Conditioned guilt (imposed by culture, family or societal pressure)
     - *Is this guilt based on disappointing others rather than doing something wrong?*
     - *Am I feeling guilty for setting a boundary or prioritising my well-being?*
     - *Would I still feel guilty if I hadn't been raised in this environment?*
     - *If my best friend were in my shoes, would I tell them to feel guilty?*

3. **Challenge the guilt narrative**
   - Now, let's question the validity of this guilt:
     - *What's the worst thing that will happen if I don't act on this guilt? (Will my world truly fall apart or is this just fear talking?)*
     - *Who benefits if I stay guilty? (Is this guilt serving me or keeping me small?)*
     - *If I let go of this guilt, what freedom would I gain? (Would I feel lighter, more confident, more in control of my life?)*
     - For example, your answers might play out like this:
       Guilt: I feel bad for not attending every family gathering.
       Reality: I am allowed to prioritise my own needs. My worth isn't based on how much I sacrifice.

4. **Reframe and release**
   - It's time to rewrite the guilt story. Pick one of these reframes or create your own:
     - Saying 'no' means I'm a bad daughter. → Saying 'no' means I respect my own limits.

- If I don't meet their expectations, I'm selfish. ➔ I deserve to live life for myself, not just for my parents.
- They'll be disappointed in me. ➔ Disappointment is their feeling to process, not my responsibility.
- Now, place your hand on your heart and say it out loud: 'I release the guilt that isn't mine to carry. I am allowed to live for me.'

5. **Action without guilt**
   - What is one small thing you can do today without guilt? (e.g. resting, saying 'no', making a decision for yourself)
   - Do it.
   - If guilt creeps in, remind yourself: *This is just conditioning. I am safe to choose me.*

Guilt is only useful when it helps us grow. When it shrinks us, it's a burden we were never meant to carry. You are allowed to exist outside others' expectations. *Now that's a piece for your puzzle.*

The story you're about to read, from Nadia (*see* the case study below), is not uncommon. It's the reality of so many women who wake up one day and realise they've been living for everyone but themselves. And when that realisation hits, it brings with it a deep, painful emptiness – one that makes it hard to see a reason to keep going and where guilt becomes an obstacle to asking for more. This is why dismantling the narrative matters: because if you don't, you risk losing yourself completely.

Case study

Loneliness and loss cause depression for Nadia

Nadia, a 50-year-old Bangladeshi woman, came to see me with severe depression. Like many South Asian women, her life centred around duty and family expectations. After she got married, she moved in with her in-laws and spent her days serving them and her husband, cooking, cleaning and fulfilling every need they had, and then, when she became a mother, looking after her children as well. At the time, Nadia didn't question this. It was simply what she had been taught to do: to serve, to give, to put the needs of others above her own.

➔

However, she didn't have any friends, she didn't go out and she felt a deep loneliness that she never spoke about. Her husband was often at work and Nadia found herself alone for long stretches of time, silently absorbing the weight of her responsibilities. Being a wife, a daughter-in-law and a mother defined her existence, leaving no room for her own needs, desires or even the chance to explore who she was outside of those duties.

Years passed and Nadia's sense of self grew smaller. The needs of her children were overriding everything else and her focus was entirely on them. Her identity was submerged by motherhood. She felt empty inside and would frequently say, 'What's the point of trying to be happy? I'm old now. No one cares. Why should I?'

As she shared her story with me, she spoke of how she longed for simple things: a new outfit for Eid, a kind word from her husband, an acknowledgement of the sacrifices she made every day. But she never received those things. Her husband never asked her what she wanted, never bought her an Eid outfit, never considered she might have desires. She gave so much of herself to everyone else, but in return, she felt unseen, dismissed. I remember a really poignant moment when she said, 'I see young boys take their wife out. My husband didn't do that. We weren't allowed', but then she immediately felt guilty for saying that.

Nadia had lived her entire life in a cycle of giving, sacrificing and feeling guilty for not being able to give even more. Now, looking back, she felt a huge sense of loss for her own life. She was just existing, like the ghost of the woman she once was. It was heartbreaking to see how much life had been drained out of her and yet no one had even noticed.

Discover your own journey

You are not bound to a rigid script. Your life is yours to shape, to create, to live authentically. It might feel like there's pressure to fit into a mould, to follow a certain plan, but I want to gently remind you that you have the freedom to discover your own journey; you don't have to follow the invisible life guide if it doesn't fit with you. You can choose to find happiness in ways that are uniquely yours, just as those before you did. Your life is yours to live, and you get to decide how to live it.

The beauty of this journey is that you get to decide what your life guide looks like. It doesn't have to be invisible any more – it can be something you create, something that reflects who you are and what you value. Most importantly, learning to embrace each step you take in life means you are taking those steps consciously and allowing the seasons of life to flow.

The 'Values exploration' exercise below will help you define what's important to *you*, in *your* life.

Exercise: Values exploration

Recognising your own invisible life guide can feel like standing at the edge of a cliff: equal parts liberating and terrifying. You might start to realise that many of the choices you've made or want to make – for example, what you study, who you want to marry, your own requirements in a spouse and how you live your life in general – have never fully been your own. Instead, they were shaped by the expectations handed down to you by your family, your culture and the society around you. How does knowing that make you feel?

One way to begin to break free from those external pressures is through a practice called values exploration. This tool helps you pause and reflect on your core values: what truly matters to *you*, not what anyone else has told you to value. It can be a grounding experience that helps you reconnect with your true self, especially when everything around you feels like it's pushing you in a different direction.

1. Start by reflecting on moments in your life when you felt truly happy, fulfilled and at peace. What were you doing in those moments? Who were you with? What aspects of those moments felt meaningful?
2. Then take a moment to list a few values that feel important to you. Not what your family or society says should matter, but what feels true to your heart. Your values could be things like freedom, creativity, independence, family, spiritual connection or self-expression.
3. Next, ask yourself: *How aligned am I with these values in my current life? Are there areas where I feel like I'm compromising these values to meet someone else's expectations? What small steps can I take to bring my actions closer to my true values?*

This tool is about clarifying your values to help you make decisions from a place of authenticity. As you move forward, you'll be able to make choices that resonate with who you are at your core, not who you've been told you should be. It gives you the courage to live in a way that feels aligned with your true self, even when that means making choices that are different from those your family or culture might expect. It's okay if this feels challenging, especially if you've been taught to prioritise others over yourself.

Finding your voice

I want you to pause for a moment and ask yourself this question: *Whose voice do I hear when I make decisions?* Maybe it's the voice of your parents or caregivers, reminding you of all they sacrificed for you, carrying with it the unspoken expectation that honouring them means living the life they envisaged for you. Maybe it's the voice of the aunties comparing you to everyone else: the girl who got married at the 'right' age, the cousin who's a doctor, the neighbour's daughter who's endlessly praised. Their voices echo in your mind, leaving you feeling like no matter what you do, you're not meeting those standards.

But what about your own voice? Can you hear it? Have you ever truly listened to it? Perhaps, over time, you learned to silence it. You pushed it to the background because wanting something different felt disrespectful. It felt terrifying, even shameful, to imagine a life that didn't follow the rules. Somewhere along the way, you were taught explicitly or subtly that having your own desires wasn't allowed, that making your own choices was selfish or impossible. So, you stopped asking yourself what you wanted, because it was easier, safer, to follow what was expected of you.

But I want you to hear this clearly: Those desires you've buried deep inside you? Those dreams that speak to you in quiet moments, the ones that you push away so quickly, begging for space to breathe? They are valid. They've always been valid. You don't need permission to want something different. You don't need anyone else's approval to imagine a life that feels like yours. So, take a moment, right now, to sit with this question: *What would I do if no one was watching?* Perhaps no one has asked you this before, but I am asking you now. What do you want? Let yourself wonder. Let yourself feel the pull of that freedom, even if it scares you. It's not selfish to wonder. It's not wrong to want. Use the 'Visibility practice' exercise on the next page to help you take your first steps.

Exercise: Visibility practice

Start small and build up gradually. Think of visibility as a muscle you need to strengthen; you don't have to leap into full visibility all at once.

- **Acknowledge your fear:** Recognise that the fear of being seen is real, especially if you've been taught to stay small or fit into a box. It's okay to feel this fear. Acknowledge it without judgement. *I am afraid of being seen and that's okay.*
- **Create space for your truth:** Find small ways to express your authentic self. This might look like sharing a thought or feeling in a conversation that you would usually keep quiet, wearing something that feels more like *you* instead of what's expected or speaking up in a group where your voice would normally remain silent. These little moments of visibility can be empowering.
- **Celebrate each step of visibility:** Every time you step into visibility, whether it's through a conversation, a decision or a creative expression, celebrate it. Recognise that each small step is a victory on your journey. You don't need to wait for a grand moment to claim your visibility – it's the small, consistent steps that make the biggest impact over time.
- **Reframe your beliefs about visibility:** If you were raised to believe that being visible was unimportant, disrespectful or even shameful, start to gently reframe those beliefs. Remind yourself that your visibility is an act of self-expression and empowerment, not selfishness. It's okay to take up space. It's not disrespectful to live authentically. It's a gift to yourself and to those around you.
- **Practice self-compassion:** It's important to be gentle with yourself as you begin this practice. There may be days when it feels too hard, too scary or too unfamiliar. On those days, treat yourself with kindness. Remember that visibility is a process and it's okay to take breaks, rest or step back when needed.

Recognising these invisible walls around you is the first step towards visibility, not by rejecting your family, your culture or your values, but by truly understanding where these expectations come from. By questioning them with curiosity rather than fear, you gain the power to choose which ones align with your truth and which ones you're ready to let go of.

You are allowed to seek joy, not just survival. You are allowed to live fully, not just endure. And your worth is not tied to how much pain you can carry. This isn't about rebellion or disrespect. It's about reclaiming your voice. It's about understanding that you can love your family and honour your culture while still living authentically. It's about realising that you are allowed to exist as more than a role, more than a daughter, a sister or a wife. You are allowed to exist as *you*. And that alone is enough.

Case study

Sameera's sacrifice and suppression

Sameera, a 40-year-old Pakistani woman, came to therapy feeling utterly run-down. From the outside, her life seemed like it was on track. She had a stable job, she was married, and she was fulfilling her role as a dutiful daughter and wife. But inside, she was crumbling under the weight of expectations she'd carried for decades.

In one of our sessions, Sameera said, her voice trembling, 'I feel like I've spent my entire life walking on eggshells. I never say what I truly feel, because I don't want to disappoint them. I don't want to be that daughter who causes shame.' She spoke about how, as the eldest child, she always took on the role of the peacemaker in the family. Whenever conflicts arose, she would swallow her opinions, suppress her emotions and play the role of the 'good daughter' to keep the family harmony intact.

But this harmony came at a cost. Sameera shared how, over the years, she sacrificed her own desires and dreams to meet the expectations of her parents. 'I never even wanted to get married so early,' she admitted during one session, and then she burst out crying. She felt shame, as if there was going to be a consequence for what she'd shared. 'I wanted to continue with my studies, but my father said it wasn't practical. And I didn't want to, because I knew how much he'd sacrificed to give us a good life. I convinced myself it didn't matter, that I was being selfish for even wanting something else.'

Her personal life was no different. Sameera had entered into an arranged marriage with a man her parents approved of, even though she had hesitations. 'He's not a bad person,' she said softly, 'but I don't feel he understands me. I don't feel like I can be myself with him. I feel like I just stepped from one set of expectations into another.' When I asked her what she wanted for herself, she hesitated. She conceded that she hadn't asked herself that question in years. 'I'm so used to putting others first,' she said, 'that I don't even know what I want any more.'

Sameera's pain wasn't just about the sacrifices she'd made; it was about the resentment that had built up over time. She felt angry at her parents for the pressure they placed on her, but she couldn't bring herself to express it. 'How can I be angry at them?' she asked, guilt written all over her face. 'They've done so much for me. How can I turn around and say that I'm unhappy? What kind of daughter does that?'

Yet, underneath the guilt, there was a growing resentment. Sameera felt trapped between all these roles. She described the pain of constantly suppressing her feelings to avoid rocking the boat. 'I'm terrified of being rejected by them,' she said. 'I feel like if I push back, they'll see me as ungrateful, as selfish. I don't know if I could live with that.'

The cost of her silence was taking a toll on her mental health. Sameera described feeling anxious all the time, waking up with a tightness in her chest that wouldn't go away. 'I feel like I'm failing at everything,' she confessed. 'No matter what I do, it's never enough. I try so hard to make everyone happy, but I feel like it's not enough.' She admitted that she'd started resenting the very people she loved the most – her parents, her husband – and then hating herself for feeling that way.

As we worked together in therapy, we began to unpack these invisible expectations that Sameera had lived under her entire life. We explored how her parents' sacrifices, while valid and meaningful, did not erase her right to have her own voice. We talked about how her fear of rejection was rooted in years of being taught that love is conditional: that it had to be earned by being 'good', by being selfless, by being perfect.

I asked her one day to imagine what it would feel like to express her true self, even if just in small ways. Her eyes filled with tears as she whispered, 'It feels selfish, but it also feels . . . free. Like I could finally breathe.'

Perhaps, as you're reading Sameera's story, you might see a little of yourself in it too. Maybe you've silenced your voice to avoid conflict. Maybe you've sacrificed your dreams to keep others happy. And maybe, like Sameera, you're starting to wonder what it would feel like to finally choose *you*.

Confronting tradition

The tension of dismantling the traditions from the invisible life guide that don't serve you is one of the hardest battles you may face. But deep down, it's okay to wonder, *Can I honour my culture without sacrificing myself?* Yes, you can, because respecting your roots doesn't mean losing yourself in them. Isn't courage in the face of change also a part of our heritage?

In your mother's world, change was a luxury she couldn't afford, not just because of the overwhelming responsibilities she carried but because the cost of change was unimaginable. If you've ever tried to have a conversation with her about dreams or desires that don't align with tradition, you might have seen the hesitation in her eyes. It's the fear of breaking something fragile: her place in the world, her identity within the community and the approval she's fought for, year after year, from people who would see change as a betrayal.

You see, your mother may have known, deep down, that she sacrificed her own happiness, her own voice. She may have even looked at you, her daughter, with both love and a sadness or jealousy. You, with your fresh dreams, your desires that didn't quite fit the mould, made her tremble. Not because she didn't love you, but because she couldn't help but wonder, *What will people say? Will I be shamed for allowing this? What will become of you if you choose a path that's different from the one I walked?*

She may not say it, but she's terrified for you. Terrified that you might be rejected – or that she might be rejected. Terrified that your pursuit of something different might lead to failure, even though you're now a grown adult. You might see how unhappy and resentful it has made her, so the confusing part for you may be the thought: *Then why do you want the same for me, too?*

It's important to understand that this fear isn't born from a place of control. It's rooted in fear and familiarity, but also in the limitations your mother has known her entire life. She doesn't know what it feels like to take that leap of faith. She never had the courage, nor the space, to question her path. And in her heart, she thinks she's protecting you from the pain she may have suffered, even if that protection comes in the form of discouraging your dreams. To her, it feels like the safe option.

Her fear of the unknown, her fear of stepping outside tradition, becomes a barrier between you and the freedom she could never allow herself. The truth is, your mother, and perhaps many of the women before her, followed the invisible life guide because it was the only thing that kept them safe – or so they thought. But was it really safe?

It was the path that kept them in the good graces of the community, that ensured they would not face rejection or shame. It was the path that demanded their obedience and self-sacrifice, because in that obedience they found a certain kind of belonging. But now, as you rise and ask for something different, something new, it shakes her to her core.

She doesn't yet know how to navigate a world where you are free to choose differently. But you, you are not bound by the same fears. You are figuring out your own path, a path that honours your desires, your dreams and your truth.

It's okay for her to feel scared. It's okay for her to not understand. But you must also recognise that your bravery is breaking down walls, not just for you but potentially for her as well. Every step you take towards your truth is a step towards liberating not just yourself but the generations that came before you. Because when they see you trusting yourself and stepping into that courage, and see you happy, they begin to trust you.

Use the 'Generational healing letter' exercise below to reflect on your mother's experiences and your own journey.

Exercise: Generational healing letter

This tool allows you to honour the sacrifices of your mother while claiming your own path. It encourages emotional release and acknowledgement of both your mother's role and your own autonomy, and helps to process feelings of guilt or fear about stepping beyond traditional paths while affirming your right to create your own future. Writing a letter provides a safe space for emotional release and generational healing.

1. **Write to your mother (real or imagined)**
   - Take a moment to reflect on your mother's journey, the sacrifices she made, the expectations she lived by and the way she shaped your path. Acknowledge her for what she carried.
   - Write a letter to your mother (whether she is alive or not), expressing gratitude for her sacrifices, acknowledging the weight of tradition she carried and understanding the fears she may have had about you stepping into a new life.

2. **Express your own voice**
   - In the second part of the letter, shift the focus to your own voice and desires. Recognise the difference between the story your mother lived and the one you are choosing for yourself.
   - Write about your own dreams, the path you wish to take and how you want to honour both your personal desires and your mother's sacrifices.

3. **Seal the letter**
   - After writing the letter, reflect on the emotions it brings up. Take a deep breath and affirm your own path. If you feel ready, you can safely destroy or burn the letter as an act of releasing the weight of generational expectations.
   - Alternatively, you may choose to keep the letter in a safe space, returning to it whenever you need to reconnect with your truth.

Earlier, I talked about those whose lives were not spoken about, who didn't fit the script provided by the invisible life guide, but whose stories mattered then and matter now. They were a reflection of life's true nature: unpredictable, messy and deeply human. The act of ignoring their stories taught us to fear imperfection, to hide vulnerability and to measure worth by compliance. And yet, those who challenged the invisible life guide carried strength. Although they were dismissed, their lives held truths about resilience, individuality and the courage to live authentically, even when it meant being unseen.

Consider how these narratives shaped the way you view success, failure and belonging. The stories that were pushed aside deserve space, not just in memory but in how we redefine what it means to live fully and truthfully. Those lives, like yours, were never meant to be hidden; they were meant to be understood. Throughout this book you will find I consistently repeat that this isn't about blame – it's about awareness. It's about recognising what was missing so you can create something different, something fuller, for yourself and the generations to come.

The truth is, breaking free doesn't have to happen in grand gestures or dramatic acts of rebellion. Real change begins in the everyday moments where you start to make small, intentional choices. These are the moments that slowly but powerfully rewrite the script. A small change might be as simple as pausing before agreeing to something and asking yourself, *Do I actually want to do this?*

Let's explore what this looks like in practice with the '10 small shifts' exercise below.

Exercise: 10 small shifts

Maybe your day starts with seeing to everyone else's needs: preparing breakfasts, mediating between Mum and Dad, being there for your siblings and endless lists ticked off before you've even had a moment to yourself. A small shift might be waking up 10 minutes earlier – not to work, but to sit with a drink and breathe.

It's about reminding yourself that your time is just as valuable as anyone else's. So, here are 10 ideas for reclaiming a piece of your day. You don't have to do all of them or do them in any particular order. Start by picking one that feels achievable, do it once and keep doing it.

1. **Wake up 10 minutes earlier:** Take that extra time for yourself – not for work, but to enjoy a quiet moment with a cup of tea or coffee, or simply for sitting in stillness.
2. **Schedule 'me time':** Carve out a time during the week where you do something just for you, whether it's reading, walking or engaging in a hobby.
3. **Practise saying what you need:** In family or work situations, gently express your needs or desires, even in small ways, like asking for space or time to relax.
4. **Create personal rituals:** Develop a simple routine that prioritises your well-being, like a short meditation, stretching or journalling every morning or evening.
5. **Change your inner dialogue:** When self-doubt creeps in or you're harsh on yourself, challenge this by reminding yourself that your voice, choices and needs matter just as much as anyone else's.
6. **Ask for help:** It's common for Brown women not to ask for help, so recognise when you need support and don't be afraid to request it, whether it's from a family member, a friend or a professional.
7. **Set an intention for your day:** It could be about prioritising joy, peace or clarity, but before getting out of bed, set a simple intention for your day.

8. **Celebrate small wins:** When you accomplish something, no matter how small, acknowledge it and give yourself credit. This could be as simple as completing a task without overwhelming yourself.
9. **Limit your 'shoulds':** Be mindful of when you say 'I should' and replace it with 'I want' or 'I choose'. Start shifting away from doing things because you feel obligated.
10. **Practice gratitude for yourself:** At the end of each day, write down one thing you are grateful for about yourself. For example, it could be your strength, your kindness or your resilience.

Perhaps you've avoided confrontation your whole life, choosing to keep the peace even when your heart felt like it was breaking. What's powerful about small shifts is that they aren't about challenging someone else but about showing up for yourself and expressing your truth. It could be as simple as saying, 'I feel hurt when . . .' or 'I need help with . . .'. These moments might feel terrifying at first, but they're acts of bravery that slowly chip away at the silence you've carried. Breaking free from the invisible life guide doesn't happen overnight, and that's okay. The guide wasn't written in a day, and it won't be dismantled in one either. But every small change you make is like planting a seed. Over time, those seeds grow into a life that feels less like an obligation and more like your own.

The 'Write your own life guide' exercise (*see* pp. 49–51) will show you how to begin.

Case study

Ayesha's constant availability

Ayesha, a 28-year-old South Asian woman, had always been the 'go-to' person in her family and circle of friends. Whether it was running errands for her parents, helping her siblings with their studies or listening to friends' problems, Ayesha was constantly available for everyone else. She felt that if she wasn't always there for others, she would be seen as selfish or neglectful, which was something she deeply feared. This constant giving left her feeling exhausted, resentful and disconnected from her own needs and desires. Ayesha wanted to explore why she felt the need to constantly be available for others and how she could shift this dynamic.

In therapy, Ayesha identified that her tendency to overextend herself stemmed from a deep-seated belief that her worth was tied to how much she could give to others. I suggested she begin with a small, practical change: taking 30 minutes each day just for herself, something that was purely for her enjoyment or relaxation, without any obligation towards anyone else.

The goal was to start reclaiming some of her time and energy for herself, with or without guilt or fear of judgement. Ayesha began setting aside 30 minutes every day in the evening, after her family's needs had been met, to do something just for herself. She started with reading a book or taking a walk, and no expectation of 'doing' anything. The key was to commit to that 30 minutes daily and allow herself to fully disconnect from any responsibilities.

After several weeks, Ayesha began noticing significant changes in both her physical and emotional well-being. The daily 30-minute break helped her feel less drained. She realised that by allowing herself this time to recharge, she had more energy to give when she chose to help others.

As she practised taking time for herself, Ayesha learned to value her own needs. She began to feel less like a caregiver and more like a person with her own desires and the right to time and space. By setting this boundary and not constantly over-committing, she felt less resentment towards others. She no longer felt like she was being taken for granted and, instead, she felt more in control of her choices.

Ironically, as Ayesha started focusing on her own well-being, her relationships with her family and friends improved. She was no longer resentful when helping them, and her support felt more genuine and sustainable. By sticking to her new routine, Ayesha began to feel a growing sense of confidence in her ability to prioritise herself without fearing she would lose people's approval.

Ayesha's story illustrates how small changes can lead to powerful transformations. By committing to just 30 minutes of daily self-care, she reclaimed her time and energy. Over time, this practice helped her set healthier boundaries, nurture self-compassion and rebuild her sense of autonomy. Ayesha's story shows that even when the urge to be constantly available for others feels overwhelming, small steps towards self-care can help shift the balance, allowing for a healthier, more sustainable way to support both yourself and those around you.

Exercise: Write your own life guide

This exercise is a gentle, step-by-step guide to help you create a life that reflects your authentic self, free from invisible expectations and rigid rules that may not serve you. It's a journey of self-discovery and empowerment, so take your time and approach each step with care.

1. **Identify your current invisible rules**

Start by re-reading this chapter carefully and reflecting on the invisible rules that control your life right now. These are the unspoken expectations that you may have internalised from your family, culture or society. They might sound like *I should be doing this* or *I must follow this path*. Take a moment to list all the rules you feel you're following right now – everything from big life decisions to small daily behaviours. This might include things like the following:

- *I must prioritise my family over my own needs.*
- *I have to follow the career path my parents want for me.*
- *I should always put on a brave face and never show vulnerability.*
- *I must get married by a certain age to avoid being judged.*

Write down as many as you can think of, but don't rush this. If you're unsure, try journalling for a bit, and the rules might come to the surface as you write.

2. **Assess and reflect on your list**

Once you have your list of invisible rules, take a moment to reflect on them. How do these rules make you feel? Are they empowering or do they feel restrictive?

Now, think about which rules you want to keep and which ones you want to challenge or let go of. But remember, this process is about the present. You don't need to make any permanent decisions; this isn't about being rigid. As you evolve, your rules may change.

To assess whether you want to keep a rule, ask yourself:

- *Does this rule align with my values and true desires?*
- *Is it helping me grow or is it holding me back?*
- *Does this rule make me feel free or trapped?*
- *How does this rule impact my mental health or sense of self-worth?*

If you feel torn about letting go of certain rules, especially because it might cause conflict with your parents or family, that's okay. The approaches suggested in the box on p. 51 may help.

3. **Letting go of the rules**

Not all rules are worth holding on to. For those that no longer serve you, ask yourself:

- How can I gently challenge this rule without creating more harm?
- Can I start with small actions that feel more manageable?
- Which rules can I let go of immediately?
- Which rules will take time to let go of?

The rules you can let go of immediately might be the small, everyday rules, like deciding not to suppress your feelings for the sake of harmony, whereas the rules that will take longer to lose might be those that involve changing the way you approach major life decisions, like career or marriage expectations. Giving yourself the space to evolve is key, though.

4. **Write your new life guide**

Now that you've reflected on your existing rules and identified the ones you want to keep or challenge, start writing your own life guide. This should reflect who you are right now, your values and what you need to thrive.

Your life guide might include things like those listed below:

- Living authentically: I will prioritise my mental and emotional health, even if it means saying no to others.
- Setting boundaries: I will listen to my own voice before agreeing to things.
- Pacing change: I will make changes in a way that feels safe for me and my family, but I won't lose myself in the process.
- Honouring my desires: I will make space for my dreams, even if they don't look like everyone else's.

Your life guide should be written in a way that's flexible, giving you the freedom to adapt. This isn't about perfection; it's about creating a plan that supports your authentic self. You're allowed to change your rules as you grow, because what feels right today might evolve tomorrow – and that's okay.

5. **Let go of the other rules**
   - Physically write down the rules you want to let go of on a separate piece of paper.
   - Reflect on each one and say aloud: 'This rule was given to me, but it is not who I am. I release it with love and gratitude.'
   - Now destroy the paper as an act of letting go; for example, tear it up or burn it safely.

> ## Addressing family pressure or cultural expectations
>
> Some rules may feel impossible to challenge; this is a reality many people face, particularly in strict, traditional households. In these situations, it's essential to minimise harm and consider the consequences of making drastic changes.
>
> Here's how you can approach this:
>
> - **Harm minimisation:** Consider whether letting go of a rule could lead to a more peaceful or harmonious situation in your household, or if it might cause more conflict, which would impact your mental health. If you sense that challenging certain rules right now would create too much tension, it's okay to take it slowly. You can work towards change in small, manageable steps that allow you to maintain peace without sacrificing your well-being.
> - **The small wins:** Some rules, like staying silent about your feelings or needs, might feel easier to challenge gradually. For example, if you've always been expected to be the 'perfect daughter' or 'caregiver', try starting with small acts of self-care that you don't need to explain to anyone. Maybe it's as simple as taking an afternoon for yourself or saying 'no' to a family request once in a while (*see* pp. 49-51 for more suggestions).
> - **Acknowledging your boundaries:** If you can't immediately let go of a rule, acknowledge it. Notice how it feels and try to communicate your boundaries with gentleness. For instance, if your family has an expectation that you work in a certain field, you might say, 'I know this career is important to you, but I'm exploring something that brings me fulfilment.' You don't have to reject their expectations completely right away; you can express your desires in a way that doesn't cause immediate conflict.

Living intentionally, not invisibly

When you begin to live intentionally, the world doesn't magically change overnight. The people around you may not notice, or they might resist this new version of you, but something deep happens within you, and you begin to reconnect with the parts of you that have been buried under years of duty and sacrifice. You start to see yourself again.

Living intentionally means making decisions because they align with your values, not because they are expected of you. When you begin to live this way, you give yourself permission to exist as more than a role - more than a mother, a daughter or a wife. You begin to exist as a whole person, worthy of care, joy and fulfilment.

As a Brown woman, living intentionally might feel selfish or even rebellious at first. But living intentionally isn't about abandoning your loved ones; it's about showing up for them more authentically. When you're honest about your needs and boundaries, you break free from resentment and exhaustion. You can finally give from a place of abundance, not exhaustion.

Instead of saying 'yes' to every request, imagine pausing and asking yourself, *Do I have the energy for this right now?* Imagine honouring that answer, even if it's a 'no'. Think about the freedom that comes with choosing how to spend your time, your energy and your love. It's not about doing less for others; it's about doing more for yourself, so that what you give is genuine and wholehearted.

Living intentionally also means allowing yourself to feel, even when those feelings are uncomfortable. It's about sitting with your sadness, anger or guilt rather than pushing those feelings aside to maintain the cover-up of being 'fine'. These emotions are messengers, telling you where you've been hurt and where healing needs to happen. By facing them, you begin to unpick the threads of the invisible life guide and slowly reclaim parts of yourself.

Perhaps one of the most beautiful impacts of living intentionally is the example it sets for others, especially your children. When they see you honouring your needs and expressing your true self, they learn that it's okay to do the same. You're not just breaking the cycle for yourself - you're creating a new narrative for them, one where their worth isn't tied to sacrifice or obedience but to their inherent humanity.

Living intentionally isn't easy. It requires unlearning decades of conditioning and confronting parts of yourself that may feel unfamiliar or even uncomfortable. But it's worth it, because as you step into this way of being, you'll find something that no invisible guide could ever give you: freedom. It's the freedom to live a life that feels like your own; the freedom to make choices rooted in love, not fear; and the freedom to finally see yourself, not as others expect you to be but as you truly are: worthy, whole and enough.

Now, with this fresh awareness, you'll discover that you possess the power to rediscover your narrative. This realisation is transformative. You are no longer obligated to follow to a script that has been handed down to you. Instead, you can consciously choose to live with intention and purpose.

Liberated from the constraints of outdated expectations, you are empowered to create a life that genuinely reflects your identity, values and worth. This is your opportunity to write a new story, one filled with intention, authenticity and a deep sense of connection to yourself and the world around you. Because, my dear Brown girls, why follow the invisible life guide and be invisible when you can live intentionally and allow yourself to be seen?

Case study

Noor's shift to living consciously

Noor, 27, had always dreamed of marriage, but for years had experienced rejection after rejection. Each time a proposal didn't work out, she felt as though something was wrong with her. One day, after another failed proposal, Noor realised she'd been seeking validation from others instead of checking in with herself. She took a step back to reflect on what she truly wanted in a marriage and focused on building her confidence. Instead of chasing proposals, she started living consciously, focusing on her passions, setting personal goals and strengthening her self-worth. As Noor shifted her mindset and let go of the pressure, she attracted more genuine connections. Eventually, she met someone who valued her for who she truly was. She found not only a fulfilling relationship but also a deeper sense of peace and confidence within herself.

Case study

Freedom from an abusive relationship for Maya

Maya, 34, was in an abusive marriage for years, too scared to leave because she feared the consequences. Despite the emotional and physical toll, she stayed, believing she had no other options. After finally gathering the courage to leave, Maya felt lost and uncertain, but she knew she had to rebuild her life. Through therapy and self-reflection, she began to reclaim her voice, set boundaries and focus on her healing. With time, Maya realised that by choosing to live consciously and putting herself first, she could create a future full of strength, independence and self-love.

2. Opening yourself up to the outside world

You may have been raised to believe that everything you do reflects on your family. If you succeed, they succeed. If you fail, they fail. And if you ever dare to cross the lines they've drawn for you, it feels like you're betraying them.

Of course, your parents' guidance is important for your well-being as you start exploring the world on your own, but what does it feel like to step out into the world, using everything you've learned from your experiences growing up and what others have taught you? That's what we're going to explore in this chapter.

The Traditional Narrative

Many Brown children are brought up with an emphasis on control and secrecy. They never question this mindset because they are raised to be loyal to their family and to tradition. It's only when they venture into educational institutions and encounter peers from different, and similar, backgrounds that they become aware of alternative family dynamics. This is also when parents and older family members begin to worry about the external factors influencing their children, fearing that as parents they may begin to lose control.

In Chapter 1, we discussed the invisible life guide you are expected to follow. Integral to that is the concept of the family, how the family is seen and how the family perceive you are seen by others in the external world. Your dreams, your choices, your voice: they all feel like they belong to the family first, because they reflect on the family. This is why so many of you feel trapped. You're constantly carrying this invisible weight of expectations, always looking over your shoulder, always wondering if you're letting someone down. It tires you out, doesn't it?

As a therapist, I've worked with countless women who tell me:

- 'My brother gets to live his life. No one questions him.'
- 'Why is it my responsibility to uphold the family's reputation?'
- 'I don't even know who I am outside of being someone's daughter, sister or wife.'

And the truth is, they're right. The rules are different for women. You're expected to follow the script perfectly: be a good daughter until you're married, be a good wife until you're a mother, be a good mother until . . . well, forever.

However, you've probably spent so much time trying to live up to the roles and expectations placed on you that you've lost yourself in the process. You've been taught to give so much of yourself to others, but in doing so, it can feel like there's no space left for *you*. You might feel like you're always being a good daughter, a good wife or a good mother, and somewhere along the way, the person you are has faded away.

Of course, that doesn't mean your family doesn't love each other, but the closeness of many Brown families can create a heavy, almost overbearing atmosphere, leaving little room for you to explore and discover who you truly are. This is known as enmeshment. In these situations, boundaries between you and your family become blurry and you constantly have to put your family's needs first, even if it means putting your own needs aside.

Living in this way can create an internal tug-of-war. You feel pulled between following what your family wants and listening to your own heart, and that can be draining. The emotional weight of enmeshment can show up in many ways. You might feel anxious, sad or simply unfulfilled in your life. You may even feel like you've actively had to suppress parts of yourself in order to keep up with everyone else's expectations.

Over time, this struggle to fit in can turn into resentment or a deep sense of disconnection from who you are. When I ask women what they want, they often pause and say, 'I don't know.' That's how deeply buried their individuality has become. Recognising that this dynamic is called enmeshment is the first step towards understanding it. We're going to dig deeper into how this commonly plays out when you want, and need, to move beyond your immediate family circle and into the outside world.

What will people say?

Be honest. How many times have you heard the phrase: 'What will people say?' It's common in South Asian families, because it's the question that dictates everything: how you dress, who you marry, where you work and even how you talk to others. What will people say if you're too loud? Too ambitious? Too different? You might not realise it, but this question probably shapes every corner of your life, from what you post on social media to how you navigate relationships.

Maybe you were taught that every decision you make has an audience, a crowd of people just waiting to judge you, so you learned early on that your life wasn't entirely your own. It was a performance, one where the stakes were impossibly high, because the neighbours, the extended family, the community, everyone was watching you and you had to get it right. This mantra becomes a prison. It keeps you from being yourself, because you're constantly afraid of stepping out of line, and many of you will have internalised it to the point where you now say it to yourself.

The phrase 'What will people say?' is used in the Brown community to pressure us, shame us and control us. Like it or not, it turns us into people-pleasers, because the fear of not pleasing and being judged is deeply ingrained in our culture. But it's not just about avoiding gossip; it's about protecting your family's honour. And it isn't just an idea; it's a weapon, used to keep you in check, to make sure you follow the rules, such as:

- **Dress the right way:** Maybe you were told to cover up or wear traditional clothing, because 'We don't want people talking' – but what they're really saying is, 'We're afraid of being judged.'
- **Speak the right way or just don't speak:** If you've ever been told to stay quiet, especially in public, it's likely because your voice was seen as a risk. Speaking your mind could draw attention, and

attention could bring shame. Don't be too loud or opinionated, because people will think they've lost control over you.
- **Follow the right path:** Whether it's your career, your choice of partner or even how you raise your children, there's always this underlying pressure to do what's expected, not what feels right for you.

It's exhausting, isn't it? To always feel like you're being watched, judged and controlled, and to always second-guess yourself because of what others might think. If you don't conform, you're not just seen as rebellious, you're seen as disrespectful. You might have heard phrases like these:

- 'You've embarrassed us.'
- 'Do you even care about this family?'
- 'What kind of daughter acts this way?'
- 'Stop acting like a man.'

These words cut deep. They make you question your worth, your loyalty, your very identity. And the worst part is, this shame doesn't just come from outside; it seeps into you. Over time, you start to police yourself.

You might feel any or all of the following:

- Guilty for wanting something different
- Ashamed for making a mistake
- Anxious about taking risks because you're terrified of failure

This constant shame keeps you small. It keeps you stuck in a box where it's impossible to grow, to explore or to simply *be*. So many of you have been conditioned to believe that the world will fall apart if you step outside the lines. Maybe you've even tried to push back, only to face resistance from your family:

- 'Why are you so disobedient?'
- 'You think you know better than us?'
- 'What will people say if you don't listen to your elders?'

These words aren't just criticisms. They're reminders that stepping out of line comes with consequences: rejection, isolation and the loss of belonging. And that's what makes this mantra so powerful. It ties your worth to the approval of others, making you feel like you'll never be enough unless you play by their rules.

As Brown women, this pressure can feel even more intense because family and community expectations are often deeply rooted in our cultures. It's natural to want to make your family proud, but sometimes this constant worry about what others will think can leave you feeling stuck, constantly anxious, abandoned or disconnected.

When you're constantly asking yourself, *What will people say?* it can have a deep impact on how you see yourself and how you live your life. Here are some ways in which this pressure might show up:

- **Self-doubt and confusion:** You may find yourself second-guessing your decisions, wondering if what you're doing is 'right' based on what others will think, even if it doesn't feel right to you.
- **Holding back your true feelings:** The fear of judgement can make you hide your emotions or experiences and keep your pain or struggles silent, because you don't want to upset anyone or bring shame to your family.
- **Constantly pleasing others:** You might feel like you have to keep giving of yourself to meet others' expectations, leaving little room for your own needs, wants or dreams.
- **Guilt for setting boundaries:** When you try to assert yourself or say 'no', you might feel a deep sense of guilt, as if you're doing something wrong, just because it doesn't fit with what others expect.
- **Feeling alone or disconnected:** You may start to feel isolated, like you can't fully share who you are with those around you, because you're always worried about how your actions will reflect on your family or community.

As a therapist, I want you to know that it's okay to feel this way and it's okay to struggle with these pressures. You've been taught to care deeply about what others think, but I want you to care about yourself, too, because your voice and your well-being matter. You deserve to make choices that honour who you truly are, even if it means letting go of the fear of judgement. It's okay to break free from that cycle, and you don't have to do it alone.

If any of this feels familiar, I want you to take a deep breath and pause. And maybe it's time to ask yourself these questions:

- *How much of my life have I lived for others?*
- *What would I do if I wasn't afraid of judgement?*
- *Who would I be if 'What will people say?' didn't exist?*

We'll be exploring some of the possible answers to these questions when we start to consider how to dismantle this narrative (*see* pp. 73–90).

Family secrets

There are many types of dysfunction within South Asian families, most of them hidden behind closed doors. Families don't want them shared due to shame, the fear of being judged and the desire to preserve the family reputation and protect the family honour, and that is why there is so much emphasis in Brown communities on keeping family secrets.

Perhaps you were raised in a home where you were repeatedly told not to talk about anything that happened within its walls. The message was that what happened within those four walls stayed within those four walls, and you had to keep up that narrative when interacting with other families or in the community.

While the fantasy of a perfect family is comforting, the reality is that every family faces unique challenges and is dysfunctional in its own way. However, the pressure to maintain an image of harmony and success is often massive, rooted in cultural expectations and societal norms. In many South Asian communities, the idea of *izzat* (honour) is huge, convincing families to project a polished exterior to the world. This facade, while seemingly protective, can lead to deeper issues that bubble beneath the surface.

In many Brown households, there can be deep-rooted dysfunctions that, while often kept hidden, affect everyone in the family. These issues can feel isolating, overwhelming and confusing, especially when you're expected to keep things within the family and protect its image. As a therapist, I want to acknowledge that these dynamics are real and you are not alone in experiencing them. Here are some common family dysfunctions I come across among my clients:

- **Addiction:** This can take many forms, whether it's alcohol, porn, gambling or substance abuse. Often, these behaviours are ignored or hidden because they bring shame to the family. You might have grown up with a parent or relative whose addiction affected the home, yet the family tried to hide it from the outside world. The emotional impact of living in a household with addiction can leave you feeling neglected, anxious and uncertain, yet you were taught to stay quiet about it, afraid of the judgement or the stigma it could bring.
- **Physical, verbal or emotional abuse:** In some Brown households, abuse is a painful reality, but it's often swept under the rug to maintain appearances. The fear of dishonouring the family by speaking up can leave you feeling trapped. You may have witnessed or experienced verbal or emotional abuse, belittling comments or harsh criticism that made you doubt your worth. Sometimes, physical abuse may be hidden or excused as discipline. You may carry scars from those moments but feel you can never truly talk about them without bringing shame to your loved ones. *See* the box on p. 63 for further thoughts on abuse.
- **Authoritarian parenting:** Many Brown families uphold a strict, authoritarian approach to parenting, where children – and especially daughters – are expected to be obedient without question. There's little room for expression or disagreement, and this often leaves you feeling like your voice doesn't matter. This strict dynamic can create feelings of fear, resentment and emotional distance from your parents, as you are taught to follow orders without ever being seen for who you really are or what you truly need.
- **Emotional suppression and lack of affection:** In many Brown households, emotions are often ignored. You were likely taught that expressing sadness, anger or vulnerability was a sign of weakness and that to maintain family honour you needed to keep those feelings to yourself. A lack of connection and affection can

leave you feeling emotionally neglected or distant from your family. You might feel like you're carrying a heavy burden of unspoken pain, unsure of who you can turn to for comfort.

- **Toxic perfectionism:** The pressure to succeed and meet high expectations, whether in academics, career or marriage, can be overwhelming. In Brown families, this pressure is often heightened by cultural norms that parallel success with the family's honour. If you don't meet these expectations, it might lead to shame or feelings of inadequacy. The constant comparison to others, and the idea that you need to be perfect, can make you feel like you're never enough and create a sense of chronic anxiety or self-doubt.

- **Unhealthy marital dynamics:** The relationship between your parents may have been filled with unresolved conflicts or unhealthy dynamics, such as a lack of communication, emotional neglect, infidelity or domestic violence. These issues are often kept behind closed doors, and you might have been expected to act like everything was fine when it wasn't. Witnessing these dynamics can leave you feeling confused or uncertain about love and relationships, unsure of what a healthy marriage or partnership should look like.

- **Cultural pressure and overbearing expectations:** Many Brown families place intense pressure on their children to conform to cultural norms and expectations, whether that's regarding career choices, marriage or maintaining traditional values. This can feel like a heavy burden, especially if your own desires don't align with what's expected of you. As a daughter, you might have been told to prioritise your family's needs over your own, leaving little space for you to explore who you really are or what you truly want out of life.

- **Lack of emotional support and validation:** While Brown families often emphasise the importance of family unity, there may have been a lack of emotional support or validation in your upbringing. You might have been told you were loved through actions (like being provided for financially) but never truly felt seen or understood. The absence of open, loving communication can create emotional distance.

Abuse: suffering in silence

This is one of the most excruciating truths to confront, so I'm holding your hands while sharing this: abuse, in all its forms, is silenced within families. You were made to believe that speaking up would tarnish the family's 'honour'. As a result, physical abuse, sexual abuse and emotional abuse all get tucked away into corners of secrecy.

If you experience abuse, you carry that burden, convinced not only that you won't be believed but also that speaking about it, and drawing attention to it, will bring shame upon everyone you love. If you draw attention to abuse, you are disrespectful; you are the shameful one. And so, you learn to stay quiet, to bury the pain deep inside, hoping it will somehow disappear.

The betrayal runs even deeper when the abuse comes from the same people you were taught to respect. Your elders, the ones who are meant to protect you, were the ones who either dismissed your pain or perpetuated it. How often were you told, 'Don't talk back; they're your elders' or 'Family comes first'?

Those words shaped you, didn't they? They taught you that respect meant silence and that loyalty meant suffering in isolation. Maybe you wanted to speak but were convinced that staying quiet was your duty, your role. Deep down, though, the pain grew. And now, even as you read these words, you may feel that knot in your chest, because the echoes of those moments are still with you.

Let me tell you this, with all the compassion I can gather: you were not wrong for wanting to speak. You were not wrong for feeling betrayed. The system that told you to stay silent was wrong. The culture that demanded your silence to maintain appearances was wrong. Your voice, your truth, has always mattered.

I am so deeply sorry you had to be alone with your experiences, but you are not alone in this pain. There are countless others who have walked this path, silenced by the same cultural rules, but silence is not the answer. Speaking up, even if it's just to yourself at first, is terrifying, I know, but your story deserves to be heard and your pain deserves to be honoured. You have permission to grieve, to be angry, to heal. You are more than the silence you were forced into. You are worthy of peace, safety and love.

Case study

Ayesha recognises the impact of sexual abuse

Ayesha, 38, grew up in a traditional South Asian family where respect and obedience were expected above all else. When she was a young girl, she experienced sexual abuse by her uncle, a betrayal that shattered her innocence and trust. When she finally confided in her mother, hoping for protection and understanding, her disclosure was met with disbelief and dismissal. The family's silence and denial became a second wound, reinforcing feelings of shame and isolation. Her mother was more focused on family ties and told Ayesha to never utter those words again.

As Ayesha grew older, the unresolved trauma from childhood lingered beneath the surface. In marriage, she faced further violation in the form of marital rape. Her husband's chilling justification – *'You're my wife; I can do whatever I want'* – reinforced her sense of powerlessness.

Ayesha did not tell anyone about what her husband did, fearing judgement, the devastating consequences of speaking out and that no one would believe her or take her seriously.

When Ayesha finally sought therapy, the focus was not just on the abuse itself but on the core wounds beneath it: the loss of bodily autonomy, the lack of consent and the internalised belief that her needs and boundaries did not matter. We centred a lot of her sessions around the following:

- **Reclaiming consent:** Learning that her body belongs to her alone, and that her voice about what happens to her body matters deeply
- **Establishing boundaries:** Understanding that boundaries are a form of self-respect, not rebellion
- **Empowering autonomy:** Building her confidence to say 'no', to feel safe in her body and to recognise her right to pleasure and respect
- **Processing betrayal and shame:** Addressing the complex emotions tied to family betrayal and cultural silence, allowing space for grief and anger without guilt

Over years of therapy, Ayesha learned to dismantle the harmful narratives she had internalised: that she was responsible, that she had to tolerate abuse and that her worth depended on others' approval.

Ayesha's story is not unique. It reflects the painful reality many South Asian women face, where cultural stigma and family denial often deepen the wounds of trauma, making it even harder to find a voice. In our communities, silence is sometimes seen as protection, but it can become a cage that traps survivors in shame, self-blame and loneliness.

Healing is possible, but it requires more than just addressing individual pain. It means gently unravelling the cultural and relational threads that hold shame and powerlessness in place. It means creating spaces where your experience is seen, believed and honoured without judgement or blame.

If you carry wounds like Ayesha's, I want you to know that your body belongs to you. Your voice matters. Your pain is valid. You deserve to reclaim your autonomy and find safety within yourself and your relationships. Therapy can be a powerful step on this journey – one that respects your culture while empowering your truth. We'll explore this further later in the chapter (see pp. 71–2 and pp. 91–5).

Rigid roles

The dysfunctions within Brown households often create rigid roles that family members fall into, which can be incredibly limiting and emotionally damaging. One particularly harmful aspect of this dynamic is the labelling of one child as the 'problem child' or 'scapegoat'. This means the family can channel all its frustrations into that person, allowing the rest of the family to avoid confronting their own shortcomings. Instead of recognising the struggles faced by the scapegoat as a reflection of the family's dysfunction, that individual is often seen as the root cause of all problems.

This scapegoating is further deepened by the common cultural practice of prioritising the collective over the individual, which can amplify the pressure on the scapegoat to conform to an idealised version of behaviour. When conflicts arise, the family points the finger at the scapegoat, reinforcing the narrative that the family functions well as long as this 'problem child' is kept in check. This pattern not only perpetuates dysfunction but also suffocates any possibility for genuine solutions or personal growth.

If you've ever felt like you're playing a certain role in your family, you're not alone. Many of us are shaped by these family dynamics, and our 'roles' can be coping mechanisms that help us get through difficult times – a way of surviving the chaos or dysfunction. Beyond the scapegoat, there are other roles (based on the Wegscheider-Cruse Family Roles Theory) that might resonate with you:

- **The caretaker:** If you're the one who's always been responsible for taking care of others, you might feel like the emotional glue that holds your family together. But taking on this role can be draining. You've likely given so much of yourself to others that it's hard to remember who you are when you're not in 'caretaker mode'. You deserve to be nurtured and supported, though, and it's okay to admit that you need care, too.
- **The hero:** Perhaps you've always felt like you had to be perfect – do well in school, be the responsible one, excel in every way – just to gain approval or feel loved. If you're the hero, it's likely that you've pushed yourself to the limit to prove your worth. But that constant pressure to be perfect can be exhausting. It's okay to be human. You don't have to be flawless to be loved or valued. Your worth is not in your achievements but in who you are as a person.
- **The lost child:** If you've taken on the role of the lost child, you may have withdrawn from the family dynamics, choosing to stay out of the way and keep to yourself. You might have felt invisible, unsure of where you fit in or how to connect with others in your family. This role can leave you feeling lonely and disconnected, but you do deserve to be seen and heard, and it's okay to come out of the shadows and find your voice again.
- **The mascot:** Maybe you've always been the one who made people laugh, used humour to lighten the mood or distracted others from the underlying pain. The mascot often hides their own pain behind jokes and playful behaviour, but deep down, there may be sadness or fear that they feel they're not allowed to show. You deserve to be more than just the person who 'lightens things up'. Your feelings are valid, and it's okay to let others see the real you, beyond the jokes and laughter.

One or more of these roles may resonate with you, but I want you to understand that they weren't chosen by you. They were ways of surviving the dysfunction you grew up with. Now, as an adult, it's time to step into your true self and free yourself from these labels and expectations. In a context where honour and reputation are fundamental, it becomes particularly important to understand the damaging effects of these dynamics, as they can strongly impact your well-being and the overall family structure.

Ultimately, these coping mechanisms uphold the family's image, but at the cost of authenticity and emotional connection. The pressure to maintain appearances and the fear of judgement creates a cycle of silence and sacrifice. However, maintaining the perfect facade, and ensuring that the extended family, such as aunts and uncles, don't gossip about your family, is tough. It can be isolating and you don't know who to talk to, because you're not really allowed to share your feelings with anyone – so, of course, you end up turning to your friends.

Suspicious friendships

The idea of having close friends outside the family is often met with suspicion in Brown families. Maybe you were told, 'Friends will lead you astray' or 'No one will ever care for you like your family does.' The message is clear: friends are temporary, untrustworthy and dangerous.

For some of you, this might have started young. Did you ever notice how your parents were always cautious about who you spent time with? You had to explain where you were going, who you were meeting and what you were doing. And even when you gave all the 'right' answers, there were still questions, raised eyebrows, the stare and maybe even an outright 'no'.

Friendships, especially deep and meaningful ones, were seen as distractions at best and threats at worst. You might have heard warnings like, 'Your friends will teach you bad habits', 'They'll turn you against us' and 'Focus on your studies, not wasting time with people who won't be there for you in the future.' What they were really saying, though, was: 'Don't trust anyone outside this house.'

The fear of friendships often comes from a place of control. Parents worry that close friends might influence you in ways they can't monitor. What if your friends introduce you to ideas or values that don't align with the family's? What if they give you the courage to question things you were never meant to question?

For mothers, especially, this fear runs deeper. The idea of a daughter forming strong emotional bonds outside the family is seen as a risk because of deeply ingrained cultural values around family loyalty, reputation and the role of women. When a daughter forms strong emotional ties beyond the family, it can feel like she's stepping away from the family's expectations or control.

The suspicion of friends is often rooted in the belief that loyalty to friends equals disloyalty to family. Spending too much time with friends, confiding in them or choosing them over family is seen as a betrayal. So, you learn to keep your friendships superficial, never letting them grow too deep or too close.

I understand that some of you may have grown up in an environment where you were discouraged from forming close friendships. It must have been difficult to hear that having friends could lead you astray. Your experiences with friends may have been overshadowed by your parents blaming them for any mistakes or decisions you made that they disapproved of, rather than your parents recognising your own agency in making choices.

No doubt your parents' fear of your friends' influence stemmed from a desire to protect you from potential harm. However, it may have overshadowed the importance of developing healthy social connections, and your parents may have unintentionally limited your ability to explore your identity and independence.

As you navigate friendships today, I can empathise with how you feel when hearing your friends from similar backgrounds share their experiences – stories that echo your own struggles and aspirations. In those moments of connection, you may feel lighter, as if a weight has been lifted due to one or more of the following:

- Shared experiences
- Emotional safety
- Understanding
- Comfort in familiarity
- Less pressure to be perfect

It's clear that healthy friendships create a space where you can express your thoughts and feelings without fear of judgement. It's important to recognise the value of being in an environment where you feel safe, heard and seen. In these relationships, your opinions matter and your voice has power.

This sense of belonging can be incredibly validating and can help you break free from the limitations placed at home. These friendships become vital not just for social support but for your emotional well-being, helping you develop a sense of self that's rooted in understanding and acceptance. As you embrace these connections, you empower yourself to navigate your journey with confidence, ultimately nurturing a healthier relationship with both yourself and those around you. But it doesn't always go that way . . . .

For some, friendships with those from similar backgrounds can be burdened with judgement and pressure. In these friendships, even the slightest expression of individuality might cause dismissive comments like, 'Don't say that' or 'That's just how your parents are.' Such reactions can reinforce a sense of inadequacy and cause you to question your own feelings and decisions. You may find yourself navigating friendships with individuals who betray your trust by sharing secrets instead of safeguarding them. This is likely to leave you feeling vulnerable and betrayed, and it is a very challenging friendship dynamic.

These friends may appear to be living within Western societal norms, but their support for traditional narratives and reiteration of the mantra 'What will people say?' probably makes it difficult to speak up, because you fear being judged. It also serves to reinforce the very traditions you perhaps want and need to confront. You may be torn between your desire to connect and your fear of losing your sense of self.

This conflict can lead to a deep sense of isolation, where your desire for acceptance overshadows your need for authentic human connection. When we experience these dynamics, it becomes increasingly difficult to find a space where we can feel seen, heard and free to express our true selves, and we crave supportive, healthy friendships that nurture rather than limit.

This idea that family is the only circle you'll ever need leaves no room for chosen family. Yet chosen family – those friends who love and support you unconditionally – can be one of the most healing parts of life. Imagine being told your whole life, 'Family is everything', then realising one day that your family doesn't understand you, can't meet your emotional needs or won't support you in the ways you need most. Where do you go then? I've worked with so many women who felt isolated because they didn't have anyone outside their family to turn to.

Case study

Jarin's stolen life

Jarin, a 33-year-old Bangladeshi woman, came to therapy and told me, 'I feel like my life isn't mine. It's theirs. And the worst part? They [my family] broke me, not the people they warned me about.' Growing up, Jarin's parents had drilled into her that family was everything and friends were nothing. Every time she tried to form a connection with her peers, her parents were quick to shut it down, painting her friends as bad influences or, worse, untrustworthy.

'They said friends would ruin me, use me and abandon me. They convinced me I didn't need anyone else, just them, so I stopped trying. I stopped answering calls. I stopped showing up.' As a teenager, Jarin wasn't allowed to go out with friends. Her parents claimed it was for her safety, for her reputation. 'What will people say if they see you roaming around with them?' they'd say.

However, at 28, she uncovered some painful family secrets and says, 'It wasn't my friends who betrayed me. It was my parents.' A financial decision her parents made in her name, without her consent, left her in debt. All her money went to clearing this debt, and they said 'no' to a marriage she really wanted. They made it difficult for her to have any choices and she describes them as controlling.

Now, Jarin feels her life was stolen from her. The friends she once had have moved on, married and built lives she feels excluded from. 'They still reach out sometimes, but I don't even know what to say any more. I don't know how to talk to them. It's been years since I shared anything real with anyone. And now... I have no one. No one to call when it feels like I'm suffocating,' she explained to me.

She blames herself for letting her parents isolate her and gets angry with herself for not being brave enough to speak up: 'You know, I used to think friends were overrated, but now I'd give anything for someone who actually *wants* to listen to me.' Jarin still lives with her parents, but resents them and barely talks to them. She yearns for connection and love.

When you read Jarin's story, you might feel a sense of sadness and really see her loneliness. As humans, we need connections – and when there aren't any, it takes a huge toll. Growing up with these ideas about friendships often leaves women feeling lonely. You might have people around you, but you don't feel truly seen or understood, because you've been told not to open up, not to trust anyone outside your family.

Maybe you've tried to build friendships as an adult, but you've found it hard to let your guard down because there's always that little voice in the back of your head saying, *What if they judge or betray me?* And then there's the guilt. If you've ever prioritised a friend over your family, whether it was spending time with them or confiding in them, you might have felt like you were doing something wrong. That's the way these beliefs linger even when you want to break free.

Ask yourself when was the last time you truly let someone outside your family get close to you? What would your life look like if you allowed yourself to build deep, meaningful friendships? Are you lonely because you've been told not to trust the very people who could bring you joy? You might want to do some journalling to help you think about these questions.

Friendship isn't a threat. It's a lifeline for so many. It's a way to connect with people who see you for who you truly are, not just for the role you play in your family. The truth is, your family can love you deeply, but they might not always understand you. That's where friends come in. They're not here to replace your family, they're here to extend it and remind you that you're never alone.

Thinking about therapy

Talk to a stranger about your problems? Share your family's struggles with someone outside the home? For a lot of you, that's unthinkable. It would be disrespectful to speak about your elders. It would feel like a huge betrayal. You would look ungrateful. And don't forget the classic line, 'But they're your parents. . . .'

Yes, they're often seen as untouchable, but just because they're your parents doesn't mean they're always right, that things don't impact you or that you should ignore your own hurt. Parents, like anyone else, can make mistakes, and loving and respecting your parents doesn't mean sacrificing your emotional well-being.

There's this deep fear that going to therapy means exposing the family's flaws: 'Why would you tell our family business to a stranger? Do you want people to think we're broken?' Admitting that you're struggling feels like admitting failure – not just yours but your parents' or even your whole family's. If something's wrong, you're told to pray harder, be patient or act like everything's fine. Admitting that you need help – or, worse, seeking it from someone outside the family – can feel like breaking some unspoken rule that this secrecy is a way of life.

If they find out you're going to therapy, people might give you a strange stare, as if something is 'wrong' with you: 'Therapy is for crazy people.' So, it's easier to pretend everything's fine, even when it's not. However, keeping everything bottled up isn't just exhausting; it's harmful. When you're taught to keep your pain private, you never learn how to express it in healthy ways. You carry it with you, day after day, until it starts to weigh you down.

Maybe you've felt this weight in your body. Maybe you have tight shoulders, a constant headache, trouble sleeping. Maybe it shows up as irritability or sadness you can't explain. Or maybe it's the sense that you're disconnected from yourself, unsure of what you need or how to heal. If you're struggling, you're essentially expected to handle it on your own, because going to therapy would be seen as weak. But secrecy and not discussing problems doesn't make them go away; it just pushes them deeper, where they grow into something harder to manage.

Case study

Sana explores the impact of her tension-filled childhood home

Sana, a 29-year-old Pakistani woman, grew up in a home where love and violence lived side by side. Her parents were respected in the community, were hard-working and always showed up to events with smiles. But behind closed doors, it was a different story.

From a young age, Sana witnessed arguments between her parents that would quickly escalate. She remembers the shouting, the sound of plates smashing, her mother's tears, the way her father's

→

anger filled the house and how terrifying it was. She learned to stay quiet and to become invisible when the tension rose.

Now, as an adult, that fear hasn't left her body. Whenever her parents raise their voices, even over something small, her chest tightens. Her hands tremble. She feels like that little girl again, frozen in place, unable to breathe. The logical part of her knows the situation isn't always dangerous any more, but her nervous system doesn't know the difference.

She began therapy in secret. No one in her family could know. 'They'd never understand,' she said. 'They'd think I'm being dramatic or disloyal.' In her community, speaking about family problems to an outsider feels like betrayal. But Sana knew that pretending everything was fine was slowly eating her alive.

In therapy, she spoke her story quietly at first. Afraid. Ashamed. Conflicted. For the first time, Sana had space to feel what she had buried for so long. She realised her anxiety wasn't random. It was a natural response to years of fear, of never feeling emotionally safe. She still loves her parents. Therapy hasn't erased the past, but it's helping her make sense of it. It's helping her feel less alone in her body, less ashamed of her truth. She's beginning to understand that healing doesn't mean rejecting your family but creating safety internally after feeling afraid for years.

Dismantling The Traditional Narrative

As a Brown woman, I know you may find it challenging to confront the traditions and attitudes your family hold in relation to the outside world, but I want you to remember that even small steps can lead to significant change. We'll be discussing the small steps you can take as we begin breaking down this traditional narrative.

Growing up in a South Asian family, the message was loud and clear: *You belong to us first*. Your identity isn't just yours; it was shaped by your family, your community and the often-suffocating cultural expectations wrapped around you. Being part of a collective culture means that your individuality probably took a back seat to togetherness, but togetherness doesn't have to erase who you are.

You can love your family, respect your culture and still claim your own space in the world. It's not about choosing between individuality and togetherness; it's about learning to balance both. And that starts with recognising that *you* matter as much as the people around you.

Exploring and healing enmeshment

I know it can be really tempting to pull away from your community, especially when things are tough. It's easy to think that the only way to protect yourself is to label your culture or community as toxic and distance yourself completely. However, doing this might leave you feeling even more alone and disconnected, missing out on the support that's still there.

The truth is, there *are* safe spaces within your community, places where you can find understanding, acceptance and meaningful connections with others. If you haven't found them yet, it's easy to believe they don't exist, but they *do*. By seeking them out, you can create a sense of belonging that lets you honour your own journey while still embracing the strength of your cultural heritage. It's not about picking only one or the other. Use the 'Community and cultural connections' exercise below to help you identify what this might look like for you.

As a therapist, at this point I want to remind you to think about the friends in your community with whom you can be vulnerable and with whom you can share parts of yourself without shame or judgement. It's so important to connect with people within your community and with people of colour, as well as people from other communities within the broader world, because there will be lots of shared experiences there.

Exercise: Community and cultural connections

The objective in the following exercise is to deepen your understanding of your relationship with your culture and community while identifying supportive spaces that nurture healing and connection:

- **Reflect on your cultural identity:** Take 10–15 minutes to write about what your culture means to you. Consider the following questions:
    - Which aspects of your culture do you cherish the most?
    - Are there traditions or values that resonate with you?
    - How do you feel when you engage with your cultural practices?

- **Identify sources of pain and joy:** Create a table with two columns, one titled 'Pain points' and the other 'Joyful experiences'. In the 'Pain points' column, list specific experiences or aspects of your community that have caused you sadness or disconnection. In the 'Joyful experiences' column, note positive moments or connections you've had within your community that made you feel accepted and valued.

- **Create a supportive spaces map:** On a piece of paper, draw a circle in the centre labelled 'My supportive spaces'. Branch out from this circle with lines to smaller circles that represent people, groups or places where you feel safe and accepted. Consider friends, family, community organisations or cultural groups that align with your values.

- **Explore outside connections and engage with new perspectives:** Over the next few months, make an effort to connect with individuals from different backgrounds or cultures. This could involve joining a cultural event, attending a workshop or simply reaching out to a new acquaintance. After each interaction, jot down your thoughts on the experience:
  - What did you learn about their culture?
  - Did you find any common ground or shared experiences?

- **Reframe your narrative:** Create a list of affirmations that celebrate your individuality while acknowledging the strengths of your culture and community. Repeat these affirmations daily to reinforce a positive mindset about your relationship with your culture and community. Some examples of affirmations are given below:
  - I honour my heritage while embracing my unique identity.
  - I can seek out safe spaces that allow me to be my true self.

When we think about enmeshment, we usually think about the negative side: feeling trapped by family expectations, having no space for yourself or not being able to express your own needs. It may seem as if your family fits the description of enmeshment perfectly, and it's true that from the outside some South Asian families might look like they're deeply enmeshed. However, just because there are aspects of your family life that seem like enmeshment, it doesn't mean everything is bad.

Family bonds are strong, and these close relationships often come from a place of deep love and respect. Our traditions and cultural values are passed down through the generations, and these strong ties to family and community help us feel connected to something much bigger than just ourselves. Being close to your family doesn't always mean losing who you are or not being able to explore other spaces; it can also mean having a support system and being part of a wonderful shared experience that carries deep meaning. Here are some ways in which this closeness can be healthy and even beautiful:

- **Emotional support during difficult times:** In times of struggle, your family may come together to offer comfort, guidance or just a listening ear. This kind of support, and knowing you have people who care and will help you get through tough moments, can be powerful.
- **Celebrating milestones together:** Whether it's a wedding, a graduation or a job promotion, your family celebrates your successes and shares in your joy. These traditions of coming together bring a sense of pride and unity that strengthens the bond you share.
- **Honouring traditions and culture:** Traditions are at the heart of your connection. From family gatherings and cultural festivals to simple daily rituals, these practices create a sense of continuity and belonging. Being part of these traditions reminds you of your roots and helps keep your culture alive.
- **Shared responsibility:** When life gets tough, your family comes together to help you, whether it's supporting you during a difficult time at work or helping out with daily tasks when you're feeling overwhelmed.
- **Shared history:** Family stories, legends and experiences that have been passed down through generations give you a sense of identity and help you feel deeply connected to your ancestors. When you hear these stories or carry on rituals, you're honouring the past while creating new memories with the ones you love.
- **Coming together as a community:** South Asian culture often focuses on community, where everyone looks out for each other. You may have experienced this sense of belonging, where your extended family or community feels like a support system,

whether you need advice, help with something or just someone to talk to. That kind of collective care is a beautiful part of our culture.

In healthy enmeshment, family isn't just about feeling overwhelmed by expectations; it's about being held, supported and nurtured, too. It's about finding strength in shared cultural practices and traditions that have stood the test of time. Yes, there can be moments when the pressure feels too much, but at the same time, these deep connections can help you grow, feel seen and never feel alone. This can give you confidence and ground you as you also explore the world outside your family and community. The 'Balance and boundaries' exercise below will help you identify the positive aspects of your family dynamic alongside those you may wish to redefine.

Exercise: Balance and boundaries

Breaking out of an enmeshed family dynamic can feel like an immense challenge. This exercise is designed to help you reflect on how enmeshment shows up in your life and how you can begin to find balance. The goal isn't to completely distance yourself from your family but to identify where you might need to establish healthier boundaries, while still embracing the beauty and love your family offers:

- **Recognise your family dynamics:** Take a moment to reflect on your family relationships. This is a chance for you to be honest with yourself about what feels overwhelming or difficult. Consider the following questions and write down your thoughts:
  - Do you feel like your needs and desires often get lost in what your family expects of you?
  - Do you find it hard to express your true feelings or opinions because you fear upsetting your family?
  - Are you often the person your family relies on emotionally, even when it drains you?

- **Identify the positive aspects of family closeness:** Your family can be a source of love and support, even if there are challenging dynamics. Consider the following questions and write down the positive moments that come to mind:
  - When have you felt supported by your family during tough times?

- Are there traditions or family practices that bring you joy or help you feel connected to your culture?
- How has your family been a source of strength or love, even when things have been challenging?

- **Set your boundaries with love:** Healthy boundaries help you maintain your individuality while staying connected to your family. Here's how you can start setting them:
  - **Say 'no' with compassion:** If you feel pressured to do something that doesn't align with your values or energy, it's okay to say 'no'. Practice saying, 'I love you and I need to take care of myself.'
  - **Create time for yourself:** Set aside time to focus on your own needs. Whether it's a quiet moment alone, pursuing a hobby or spending time with friends outside of family, this time is for you.
  - **Communicate honestly:** Be gentle but clear when expressing your feelings. If something is bothering you, share it in a calm and honest way, without fear of rejection. For example, 'I feel overwhelmed when [situation] happens and I need space to process it.'

- **Celebrate your cultural connection:** It's important to remember that family, culture and tradition are beautiful parts of your identity. Here's how you can embrace that connection while maintaining your boundaries:
  - **Honour your traditions:** Engage in cultural practices that feel meaningful to you. Celebrate holidays or rituals that connect you to your heritage, while also creating space for your own personal growth.
  - **Share your culture with others:** Sometimes, sharing stories or traditions with others outside your immediate family can help you honour your culture while expanding your understanding of it. This helps you integrate your cultural identity in a way that feels authentic to you.

- **Reflect on your progress:** Once a week, take some time to reflect on how you're doing with setting boundaries and

honouring both your family and your individuality. Write down any thoughts, feelings or changes you've noticed. Give yourself credit for the progress you've made, no matter how small:
- How are you feeling emotionally? Less drained? More connected to yourself?
- Are there moments when you're still struggling to maintain boundaries? What might you do differently next time?
- How does it feel to celebrate the positive aspects of family and culture while also creating space for yourself?

Our cultures and traditions offer us something unique: a sense of belonging, a place to be understood and a beautiful way to carry on the legacy of those who came before us. It's this bond that can help us thrive, knowing we have a support system that goes beyond just the individual. Healthy enmeshment, when balanced, gives us both the space to grow individually and the comfort of family and culture to lean on. So, why be torn between both?

You may well be feeling the weight of wanting to choose your own happiness while also longing for that deep sense of community. It can be painful to consider distancing yourself from those you love. You might think, *How can I just let go of my cousin who brings so much joy into my life, even if she doesn't fully understand my choices?* Or you might worry, *What about my grandmother, who calls me every Sunday to share her wisdom and love, even if it sometimes feels heavy?* The potential cost of the choice can feel immense. Use the 'Reconnecting with community' exercise below to reflect on how to find the right balance for you.

Exercise: Reconnecting with community

Now, as you seek your own happiness, you might feel a deep sense of loss, but it's okay to want to forge your own path while also yearning for the comfort of those deep connections. The balance between your individuality and your community will probably be a delicate one, but reflecting on the following questions will help you find it:

- **How do you feel when you think about your community?** Do you feel supported or do you feel disconnected? Write down how you really feel.

- **Have you ever wanted to pull away from your community?** If so, why? Write down what made you feel like this. And if not, why?
- **Are there people or places in your community where you feel safe and understood?** Think about any friends, groups or places where you feel accepted. Write about these safe spaces.
- **If you don't feel like you have these spaces yet, what would they look like to you?** Imagine how a safe, supportive space would feel. Write down what it would be like.
- **What would it be like if you saw your community as a place of strength, not just obligation or pain?** Write down what would make your community a positive space for you.
- **What small step can you take to make this happen?** Maybe it's reaching out to someone, attending a group event or simply looking for a supportive space. Write down one small step you can take.

So, how do you move forward, addressing the issues that aren't serving you while still retaining the positives? Let's start by breaking down the mantra 'What will people say?'

Deconstruct the mantra

What is it that you fear when you ask yourself, *What will people say?* You fear being judged. You fear the shame of not meeting other people's expectations. When you grow up hearing this question, you internalise that shame, which makes you see yourself as a 'bad' human. This shame can show up in so many ways:

- You doubt yourself before you even try something new.
- You feel unworthy when you don't meet certain cultural standards.
- You shrink yourself to avoid standing out, even when standing out would make you proud.
- You continue to stay invisible.

Read this out loud: shame was never mine to carry. It was handed to you by a culture that prioritises appearance over authenticity. It was passed down by generations who didn't have the tools to break free from it themselves. The only way to control you was by shaming you. Letting go of shame starts with understanding that you're not responsible for other people's opinions. Your worth doesn't come from their approval; it comes from within you.

Letting go of *What will people say?* is not an overnight process. Here are a couple of ways to start:

- **Challenge the narrative:** Every time you hear that voice in your head asking, *What will people say?* pause and ask yourself, *Whose voice is this?* Is it really yours, or is it the echo of years of conditioning? By recognising that this fear isn't truly yours, you can start to separate yourself from it.
- **Practice self-compassion:** Letting go of this fear doesn't mean you'll never feel it again. There will be moments when it creeps back in, and that's okay. Be kind to yourself in those moments. Remind yourself that growth is messy and that you're allowed to take your time.

Imagine a life where *What will people say?* doesn't control you. A life where your choices reflect your desires, not your fears. A life where you can embrace who you are without apology. Because the truth is, the people who truly love you want to see you happy. And the people who judge you? Their opinions were never your responsibility in the first place.

Let's look at a practical way to get started with the 'Create your real audience and find your voice' exercise below.

Exercise: Create your real audience and find your voice

I think it's fair to say that shame isn't something many of us can just let go of, yet it is something we can manage. So, instead of worrying about the imaginary audience, it's about thinking about the real audience. This exercise will help you focus on that:

1. **Sit with yourself:** Find a quiet space where you can be alone with your thoughts. Take a few deep breaths to ground yourself.
2. **Draw a circle:** On a piece of paper, draw a circle and label it 'My real audience'.
3. **Identify your real audience:** Think about the people whose opinions truly matter to you. These are the people you trust, respect and feel comfortable sharing your thoughts with. Write their names in the

circle. These are the people who you value and whose feedback aligns with your values.

4. **Create a second circle:** Draw another circle around the first one. Label it 'My voice'.
5. **Reflect on your values and opinions:** Inside the 'My voice' circle, write down your values and your core beliefs. What matters most to you? What are your thoughts and opinions that come from within rather than being influenced by others? This is where you define *you*.
6. **Align your audience with your voice:** Reflect on how the people in your 'My real audience' circle align with your values and opinions. Are there areas where their opinions support your voice? Are there any places where you may need to stand more strongly in your own beliefs?
7. **Empower yourself:** Remind yourself that you are in charge. While you can value the opinions of those in your 'My real audience' circle, *you* hold the final say in your life. You are the one who gets to decide what feels right for you.
8. **Take action:** This week, practice honouring your voice and the opinions of your real audience. Stand firm in your values while allowing yourself to remain open to feedback from those who truly matter.

As humans, we need to connect with one another, so of course we value the opinions of the people with whom we have relationships. With this exercise, I am inviting you to think about who these people are and to value what you yourself think as well as what they think.

Letting go of *What will people say?* is an act of courage, and it's so liberating. It's a statement that your life is yours to live, your story is yours to write and your happiness is yours to claim, which is the kind of success no one can take away from you.

Friends: Our chosen family

As we discussed earlier, growing up you were constantly told that family is everything, but it's likely your friends know things about you that your family doesn't – things your family may never have asked about or simply don't want to know about you. Just because someone is family doesn't necessarily mean they know you well, so it's quite possible to feel your friends understand you better than members of your family do.

Real, supportive friendships can bring so much healing and joy. Having friends outside your family who truly care for and support you can feel like a breath of fresh air. Friends can make you feel accepted and loved for who you really are, and they can encourage you to chase your dreams and express yourself freely, so let me show you how to manage your friendships.

We'll start by looking at the nuances of what you heard your parents say about friendships. Parents usually act out of love and a desire to protect you, but sometimes their fears can make them overprotective. For example, they may have set strict rules to keep you safe because they were worried about the world, or perhaps they warned you not to get too close to friends because they were genuinely afraid those friends could hurt you emotionally or lead you astray.

If your parents were cautious or disapproving about friendships, it may have made you hesitant or distrustful when it comes to forming meaningful relationships outside the family. However, it doesn't have to be this way. You don't have to reject your parents' views outright, but nor do you need to accept them blindly. What if, instead, you reframed them in a way that serves you? As an adult now navigating your own life, the quality of your friendships matters deeply, and you have the ability to choose connections that uplift, support and inspire you.

A quick way to assess the value of your friends is to ask yourself the following questions:

- *How do I feel when I leave a space with my friends?*
- *Am I energised, understood and valued by my friends?*
- *Or do I feel drained, judged or like I'm shrinking into someone I don't recognise?*

Remember, language is powerful. The way in which your parents framed their warnings about friends likely came from many places, but it may have missed the mark because of differences in experience and understanding. Your generation communicates differently, views relationships differently and faces a unique set of challenges and opportunities. This doesn't mean rejecting your parents' lessons entirely. You can honour their wisdom while also creating a narrative about friendships that fits your life, your values and your needs.

The conversations you engage in with your friends, the energy you exchange and the values you align with all shape the lens through which you see yourself and the world. If your friendships are filled with gossip, comparisons and negativity, it's natural that those energies will seep into your beliefs about yourself. But if your friendships are rooted in support, honesty and growth, you'll find yourself thriving in ways you didn't even know were possible. 'The friendship checklist' exercise below will help you identify the impact different friendships have on your life.

Exercise: The friendship checklist

I encourage you to look at your friendships through a mindful lens. Evaluate them not with the suspicion that may have been passed down to you but with clarity and self-respect. It's not about cutting people out of your life because they don't conform to some ideal, but rather recognising when a friendship has run its course or when boundaries need to be adjusted. Use this checklist to evaluate how well a friendship aligns with your values and needs:

- **Support:** Does this friend offer emotional support when you need it or is it one-sided? Are they judgemental? Do they have empathy?
- **Respect:** Do they respect your boundaries, time and opinions?
- **Trust:** Can you rely on this person to keep their word and be there for you when needed?
- **Encouragement:** Do they uplift you and encourage you to be your best self?
- **Shared values:** Do you share similar values or is there mutual respect of your differences?
- **Balance:** Is the friendship balanced or do you often feel drained or overwhelmed?

At the end of the day, your friendships reflect the relationship you have with yourself. The more you honour your worth, the more likely you are to surround yourself with people who honour it, too. Take a moment to reflect on your own values and what you're seeking in friendships:

1. **Identify your core values:** Write down the three to five things that are most important to you in life (e.g. honesty, loyalty, kindness, independence, etc.).
2. **Reflect on your current friendships:** Look at your closest friendships. Do they align with these values? Are they making you feel respected and supported?

3. **Ask yourself these questions:** *How do I feel when I'm with this friend? Do I feel heard and understood? Do I feel drained or energised after spending time with them?*
4. **Adjust your circle:** If a friendship doesn't align with your values or leaves you feeling unhappy, it may be time to re-evaluate that friendship.

It's important to take the time to reflect and to choose, because the people you let into your life hold immense power: they can either help you grow into the best version of yourself or keep you stuck in cycles that don't serve you.

ARE YOUR FRIENDS SERVING YOU?

You might find yourself in friendships where you feel like you must shrink yourself to fit in, where there's subtle or even overt competition, leaving you questioning your worth after every interaction. Or maybe you're in friendships where you can't show up as your authentic self, where judgement is like a constant feeling. These aren't just passing feelings; they're heavy burdens that chip away at your sense of self over time. You might find yourself staying in these friendships out of habit, fear of loneliness, the longevity of the relationship or a belief that this is just how it's supposed to be. If your friendships are draining you rather than replenishing you, it's worth pausing to reflect on whether they're aligned with your well-being.

Here's what unhealthy friendships look like:

- **Lack of mutual respect:** One person's opinions, feelings or boundaries are consistently ignored or belittled.
- **Emotional imbalance:** One friend consistently takes more emotionally than they give, leaving the other feeling drained.
- **Unreliable behaviour:** They frequently cancel plans, fail to follow through on promises or are unavailable when you need them.
- **Frequent drama:** There's constant conflict, misunderstandings or unnecessary drama that leaves you feeling unsettled.
- **Jealousy and competition:** They compete with you instead of supporting your successes, or they feel envious when things go well for you.
- **Lack of support:** They don't celebrate your achievements and may even downplay or criticise your successes.

- **Negative influence:** They encourage unhealthy behaviour or choices, like enabling bad habits or encouraging you to act in ways that don't align with your values.
- **Taking advantage:** They expect you to always be there for them but rarely offer help or support in return.
- **Guilt tripping:** They use guilt or manipulation to get you to do things you're uncomfortable with or don't want to do.
- **Tendency to control:** They try to control your decisions or dictate what you should or shouldn't do, especially when it comes to your personal life or making other friends.

The way in which you approach friendships is likely influenced by what you've observed in the relationships of those around you. Maybe you've seen your mother hold on to relationships where kindness and trust feel absent. She might tell you about a certain auntie or family friend she doesn't trust, yet she continues to engage with them because that's what's expected.

The irony is, you might find yourself in similar situations with your friends, ignoring the red flags because you feel letting go would disrupt the balance or invite judgement. Your mother might struggle to understand the dynamics of your friendships, just as you might find it hard to grasp why she tolerates certain toxic relationships within her circle. She might criticise the way your friends behave, and you might find yourself doing the same about hers. The truth is, both of you have different experiences, but the pain of unhealthy relationships is the same.

Use the 'Identifying friendship patterns' exercise below to reflect on the rules you may have internalised around friendships.

Exercise: Identifying friendship patterns

When you reflect on the parallels between your mother's friendships and your own using the tool below, you might begin to notice how much of your discomfort stems from unspoken rules and inherited patterns. This awareness is powerful because it allows you to break cycles. You can start asking yourself the tough but necessary questions: *What do I need in my friendships? Who do I become when I'm around certain people?* In the end, it's about choosing a tribe that feels true to you; this exercise will help you do that:

1. **Observe your mother's friendships:** Think about how your mother interacts with her friends:
   - Does she have close friends or more distant ones?
   - How does she handle conflicts with her friends?
   - Is she emotionally open with her friends or does she keep things private?

2. **Compare her friendships to your own:** How do your friendships look in comparison?
   - Do you have similar behaviour patterns, like keeping friends at a distance or avoiding conflict?
   - Are you emotionally available to your friends or do you hold back?

3. **Reflect on family influence:** How has your family's view of friendships shaped your view?
   - Were friendships treated as important in your family or were they often overlooked?
   - Did you see healthy or unhealthy friendship dynamics growing up?
   - How does that manifest in your own friendships?

4. **Identify patterns you want to change:** Do you see any patterns from your mother's friendships that you don't want in your own life?
   - For example, if your mother tends to keep friends at a distance, would you like to work on being more open and vulnerable?
   - Or if you've seen your mother not say anything when mean comments are made towards her, then you might choose to build the courage to tell your friends when they're being insensitive.

5. **Take action:** Think about one small change you can make to build healthier friendships. For example:
   - What can you do to open up more? e.g. start naming emotions instead of using 'I'm fine', 'I'm good' or 'I'm OK'; check in with one friend and ask them if they have have five minutes for you to share something small.
   - What do you need from friendships? e.g. time, meet ups, a listening ear, laughter, a distraction.
   - How can they serve you, or how can you take up space in these friendships? e.g. allow yourself to receive their friendship; stop silencing yourself; say if you want consistency.

This is where the idea of a *chosen family* comes in. A chosen family isn't about replacing your biological one; it's about expanding your circle by adding people who truly get you. These are the friends who show up for you and who love you for who you are, not who you're expected to be. They're the ones who remind you that you're not alone, even when it feels like the world is against you.

Your chosen family can be the ones who remind you that it's okay to want more. They're the ones who cheer for you when you're too afraid to cheer for yourself. They're the ones who say, 'I've got you' when everything feels like it's falling apart. And the best part? You get to decide who's in your chosen family, just like you decide whose opinions matter. It's not about who you're supposed to love; it's about who loves you back in the way you deserve.

Trusting someone outside your family can feel strange at first, particularly if you grew up being told not to trust friends, and I understand that you might hesitate initially. However, I encourage you to trust and make friendships, because when you let people in, you create a space for connection that's built on love, not obligation. The 'Reflections on friends and family' exercise below will help you begin.

Exercise: Reflections on friends and family

Working through and reflecting on the following questions will help you open up to finding those rare souls who don't just tolerate your truths but celebrate them:

- **Have there been times when your friends have helped ease your loneliness?** Think about a specific moment when a friend helped you feel less alone. What did they do or say that made you feel more connected?
- **What are the benefits of having friends who understand you, especially when family dynamics are strained?** In what ways have friendships been a source of comfort or support when you've felt unsupported by family?
- **How do you feel when you don't have a close connection with family?** Explore your emotions and the impact this has on your mental health and sense of belonging.
- **What do you think is the role of friendships when family relationships are challenging or strained?** Consider how friends

can fulfil a need for connection and understanding when family might not provide that support.
- **Are there areas in your life where you could invest more time in cultivating meaningful friendships?** Think about whether there are friendships that could use more attention or if there are new opportunities for connecting with others.
- **What qualities do you look for in a friend?** What characteristics are important to you in a friend (e.g. trustworthiness, empathy, shared interests)? How might you find or nurture friendships with these qualities?

Building friendships with people from different races, cultures and ages can be a beautiful way to grow and learn. As a Brown woman, it's natural to seek connection with others who share similar experiences, but opening yourself up to diverse friendships can bring so much more. When you connect with people from different backgrounds, you can learn about new cultures, traditions and ways of thinking. These friendships help you see the world in a bigger way and can teach you things you never expected.

Your chosen family is your chance to recreate what family means, on your terms. It's your opportunity to construct a support system that lifts you up instead of holding you back.

With your chosen family, you can show up as your whole self, flaws and all, and still be met with love – but I must remind you this is only the case if your conditioning doesn't bleed into those friendships. The only way to know that is through self-awareness; the 'Examine the dynamics' exercise below is designed as a starting point. Otherwise, the cycle continues and you end up playing the same roles with your friends that you play with your family.

Exercise: Examine the dynamics

Let's slow down and reflect together. I know how heavy it can feel to carry the weight of everyone's expectations while also trying to stay true to yourself. Sometimes, we're pulled in so many directions by all of our relationships, including our friendships, that we forget to pause and ask ourselves, *But what do I actually feel? What do I actually need?* This next exercise is a gentle invitation to come back to yourself: to reflect with honesty, without judgement, and to notice how your relationships, values and voice are showing up in your life right now.

Take your time as you work through the steps below. Breathe. There's no right or wrong here, just your truth, and that's more than enough.

1. **Reflect on your relationships:** For example, in answer to the question, 'What do you appreciate about your friends?' you might say, 'I love how Aisha always listens without judgement and how Rina makes me laugh even on tough days. What would I like to change? Maybe I feel Habiba often shares my secrets with others, which makes me uncomfortable.'
2. **Practise active listening:** You might begin with an opener like, 'I want to hear more about your thoughts on this. Can you tell me more about what you think?' After the other person shares, you might say, 'So what I'm hearing is that you feel frustrated about the situation. Is that right?' This shows you're engaged and trying to understand their perspective.
3. **Identify your values:** For instance, you could formulate this as, 'I value honesty, so I want to surround myself with friends who are open and truthful. I also value respect, which means I want to have friendships where we support each other's choices, even if they differ from our families' expectations.'
4. **Reframe your judgements:** If a friend says, 'You're acting so Westernised,' you might reframe it as, 'I'm exploring what feels right for me and that's okay. It's important for me to balance my culture with who I am.' If a family member asks, 'What will people say?' you can respond, 'What matters most is how I feel about my choices, not just what others think.'

When you've completed this reflection, hold what comes up with kindness.

You know that by choosing to prioritise your well-being, you may be seen as the outsider, the one who disrupts the harmony of togetherness. As a Brown woman, completely cutting the ties with your family and your community is not necessarily the go-to solution, so let's talk about therapy.

Therapy: A resource for everyone

I want to encourage you to think about therapy in a new light. Therapy isn't just for those with a mental health diagnosis. Every single person can benefit from therapy. I know taking that first step feels daunting. It's normal to feel overwhelmed at the thought of sharing your experiences of growing up, talking about your parents, siblings, parents or friends or expressing feelings you've tucked away for so long. You might feel like you're betraying your family or your community by seeking help, and I understand that pressure, but I'm here to remind you that acknowledging your feelings doesn't mean you're turning your back on those you love.

Therapy is about freeing yourself from the burden of carrying your feelings alone. It's an opportunity to unpack the experiences that have shaped you, to find clarity in the chaos and to reclaim parts of yourself that may have been hidden for too long. Imagine the relief of releasing those emotions, of finally giving yourself permission to feel without fear. This journey may be challenging, but it's also an invitation to embrace your own discovery. You deserve to explore your inner world, to understand your emotions and to build a life that feels authentic to you.

The journey into therapy may take many forms, and it's important to recognise that everyone's path is unique. Some of you might choose to see a White therapist, believing it will feel safer, because they won't recognise your family or know anyone in your community. After all, a therapist from your own culture will represent the very society you navigate every day, and you might worry that they'll see you through a lens of shared beliefs and cultural norms that don't resonate with your own experiences.

However, if you opt for a therapist who doesn't share your cultural background because it seems like a safer choice, you may quickly realise that, while the lack of familiarity can feel comforting, it can also create a disconnect. Your therapist might struggle to understand certain cultural nuances and you may find yourself having to explain aspects of your life that should be inherently understood.

This gap can lead to moments where your therapist's suggestions feel impractical or even impossible. You might find yourself feeling frustrated, thinking, *How can I disconnect from my family when they're* such an integral part of who I am? Additionally, you may notice subtle judgements towards the very aspects of your cultural traditions that you cherish and value. This realisation can create a sense of unease as you begin to question whether your therapist truly appreciates your whole self, including the parts of your culture that are so meaningful to you.

When therapy starts to feel unsafe, it can become a barrier to your growth. You might feel trapped between wanting to be understood and fearing that you won't be accepted as you are. These feelings are valid and should be acknowledged and explored, because you deserve a therapeutic relationship that honours your entire identity and where you can share your experiences without fear of judgement or misunderstanding.

It takes immense courage to choose a therapist who looks like you. The fear can feel overwhelming, especially when all those doubts about picking a Brown therapist resurface, but imagine the moment you connect with a Brown therapist. When you find someone who understands your cultural context and creates a safe space for you, you will start to feel your authentic self emerging. Your inner child, who may have felt neglected or unprotected in the past, will begin to feel safe for the first time. It's like unlocking a door to parts of yourself that you thought were forever closed off.

The remaining exercises in this chapter (see below) are designed to help you embark on your therapy journey with confidence.

Exercise: Reflect on how you feel about therapy

Start by thinking about your current feelings towards therapy. It's okay if you feel nervous, hesitant or uncertain. These emotions are valid, and by identifying them, you can begin to gently challenge any limiting beliefs you might have. This is your space to honestly acknowledge how you feel about the idea of therapy, so write down whatever comes to mind, without judgement:

- What thoughts or feelings come up when you think about therapy? Are you afraid, doubtful or maybe even embarrassed?
- Do you feel that seeking therapy means there's something wrong with you? Why or why not?
- Do you have concerns about how others in your family or community might react if you went to therapy? What are those concerns?

Exercise: Challenge the myths about therapy

It's important to recognise that therapy isn't just for people with mental health issues. It's for anyone who wants to understand themselves better, heal from past wounds or navigate difficult emotions. By challenging the myths, you'll start to shift your perspective and reduce any fears or doubts about therapy. Writing these myths and truths down isn't just an exercise, it's a way of gently reprogramming the stories you've absorbed. When we put things into words, we engage both our conscious and unconscious minds. This act of writing helps embed new beliefs into our awareness, challenging internalised stigma. By actively challenging these myths, you're not just learning, you're beginning to shift your mindset, reducing internal resistance and opening up to the possibility of healing.

So now, write down these myths and their corresponding truths:

- **Myth 1:** Therapy is only for people with serious mental health problems.
    - **Truth:** Therapy can be for anyone, no matter how big or small the issue may seem. It's about learning to cope with life's challenges and gaining emotional clarity.
- **Myth 2:** If I go to therapy, I'm betraying my family or community.
    - **Truth:** Seeking therapy is not about turning your back on your loved ones. It's about taking care of yourself so you can show up better for them.
- **Myth 3:** I should be able to handle everything on my own.
    - **Truth:** It's okay to need support. Everyone deserves help when navigating difficult feelings and therapy can provide that safe space.

Exercise: Visualise therapy as a healing tool

Take a moment to picture yourself in a therapy session. Imagine it as a safe, welcoming space where you are heard and understood. Visualising therapy as a tool for healing can help you see it as a positive and empowering step and prepare you to take that first step. Write down your visualisations and reflect on the feelings that come up:

- How would it feel to talk openly about the experiences and emotions you've been carrying with you?

- Imagine leaving a therapy session feeling lighter or more at peace. What kind of relief do you think that would bring you?
- Can you picture yourself feeling proud of taking this step to care for your mental and emotional health?

Exercise: Setting small, achievable goals for seeking therapy

If you're still feeling unsure about therapy, take the process one step at a time. Set small goals that feel manageable and empowering. That way, you can start moving forwards without feeling overwhelmed. Even the smallest action is progress. Using the following examples, write down your first goal and take a small step today towards making it happen:

- **Goal 1:** Research therapists in your area or look into online therapy options.
- **Goal 2:** Talk to a trusted friend or family member about your desire to try therapy.
- **Goal 3:** Reach out to a therapist and schedule a first session, even if you're not sure what to expect.
- **Goal 4:** Journal your feelings about therapy and keep track of how your thoughts and emotions shift over time.

Exercise: Practice self-compassion

Finally, remind yourself that it's okay to need help. You are deserving of care and support, just as much as anyone else. Therapy is a way for you to invest in yourself and your well-being. Be kind and patient with yourself as you consider this new step towards healing.

Here are some affirmations on the importance of self-compassion for you to read out loud:

- I deserve to take care of my emotional health.
- Seeking therapy doesn't mean there's something wrong with me. It means I'm being proactive about my well-being.
- It's okay to feel unsure about this process. Taking it one step at a time is all I need to do.

This journey is about reclaiming trust, both in yourself and in others. You'll start recognising that healthy relationships can exist, whether with friends, family or even romantic partners. The process of healing will become clearer as you navigate these new, positive experiences, while each conversation with your therapist will help you break down those barriers, allowing you to approach your community with a fresh perspective.

Therapy is not selfish. You've learned to hide parts of yourself. You've learned to settle, to shrink, to smile through the pain. There's a grieving process that comes with this kind of suppression. The more you hide, the more invisible you become – to others, yes, but, more importantly, to yourself. It might finally be time to be seen.

3. Marriage, in-laws, divorce and stigma

In *Bridgerton*, arranged marriage is openly and positively discussed. *Married at First Sight* and *Love Is Blind* are the same. Yet, not long ago, South Asian women who went through arranged marriages were considered oppressed and seen as being forced into a union they had no choice about. There is a huge difference between an arranged and a forced marriage, which I will talk about later in this chapter, but for now let's begin by looking at traditional ideas about marriage within the South Asian community.

Many young girls are understandably excited about getting married and the prospect of their wedding, but the anticipatory conversations about the venue, the guest list, the outfit and so on lead them to believe that this will be their fairy tale – that it will bring joy and that they will finally get their happily ever after. Of course, some people do get their happily ever after, although some people don't; however, this not only keeps girls living for the future instead of enjoying the present but also creates an incredible weight of expectation around marriage.

When I was young, I didn't really understand my family's beliefs and traditions around marriage, and I found that lack of understanding bewildering and disempowering. Perhaps you felt the same? Marriage has many layers for Brown girls, so let's begin to unpack some of these and understand the complexities.

The Traditional Narrative

Let me take a guess here, my Brown girls: your elders have joked about you getting married for as long as you can remember. That's because when a baby girl is born, everyone assumes they know how her life will turn out. Her father will look after her until her husband does. By a certain age, she will get married. Yes, she'll go to school, and yes, she can study, but once she reaches a certain age, it's time for her to marry. Because marriage is the ultimate goal.

As you were growing up, you probably went to weddings and were told, 'You're next', but it's not only your family – it's the entire culture. Marriage isn't just a milestone in South Asian communities; it's often presented as the *whole point of your life*. Even people who are in unhappy marriages tell you to get married. And let's not forget, it's not simply the pressure to marry but the pressure to marry *right*: the perfect guy from the perfect family with the perfect job.

Being perfect to secure a marriage

You were likely told, directly or indirectly, that your education, career or any dreams you had for yourself were important, but only as long as you didn't ignore the *real* goal: finding a husband. Maybe you heard comments like, 'What's the point of all this studying if you're not going to settle down?' or, worse, 'You don't want to be too ambitious – men don't like women like that.'

Think back to how early this started for you. Perhaps as a teenager you were warned to 'behave properly' so you would be ready for your future in-laws. Maybe your every move was inspected to ensure you'd be seen as 'marriage-worthy'. The way you spoke, the way you dressed, even the way you laughed – everything was assessed for how 'marriageable' you were.

Whether it was through the stories you were told, the lessons you were taught or the casual remarks from relatives, you were probably introduced early on to this ideal of the bride who is graceful, accommodating, skilled in running a household, and, above all, *pleasing* – to her husband, her in-laws and society. And the idea of becoming the perfect bride, wife and daughter-in-law wasn't just something you heard about; it was baked into your upbringing, and the pressure to be prim and proper must have weighed heavily on your shoulders.

How many times have you stood in front of a mirror fighting back tears, hidden when aunties came over because you were afraid of their criticism or skipped meals in an effort to conform to their standards? Were you told to keep your weight *in proportion*? No doubt the subtle or sometimes not-so-subtle comments came from family members, neighbours or even people in the community, each reinforcing the idea that your body wasn't your own but rather something to be moulded and judged by the world in order to obtain a suitable husband.

Then there's the obsession with 'fairness'. The idea that beauty only exists in a lighter complexion reaches into every corner of life. It's in the advertisements, the comments made at family gatherings or the comparisons made to cousins or friends. Maybe you tried fairness creams or avoided the sun, not because you wanted to but because the world around you insisted that lighter skin would make you more desirable, more lovable, more worthy. But deep inside, each comment, each rejection of your natural beauty, chipped away at your self-esteem.

However, let's acknowledge that not all of it is bad, and many of the lessons taught in the process of preparing Brown girls for marriage come from a place of love and care. For example, consider the following:

- **Respect and humility:** Learning to respect others, especially one's elders, is deeply rooted in South Asian culture. It nurtures connection, warmth and a sense of community.
- **Life skills:** Cooking, cleaning and managing a household are skills that can be empowering. They're not inherently about submission; they can be about independence and self-sufficiency.
- **Grace and composure:** Learning to handle situations with dignity and patience can be an asset in life, not just in marriage.

These qualities, when imparted in a balanced way, can serve you well in many aspects of life. The problem, though, lies in how these lessons are often framed: not as tools for your growth but to benefit others and to make you 'worthy' of marriage.

Being perfect at serving someone else can take a toll on your mental health in ways that are often hard to recognise. You might feel a constant need to prove yourself, even when no one is watching. You might feel resentment, knowing that your worth is being tied to how well you fit into someone else's mould. You might struggle with feelings of inadequacy, believing you'll never live up to the ideal.

And what happens when you make mistakes? Because you *will* make mistakes – after all, you're human:

- You might wear something your in-laws deem inappropriate.
- You might disagree with your husband.
- You might not spend the 'right' amount of time with him or his family.
- You might not be able to make sacrifices in the way they want you to.
- You might cook differently from them.
- You might not keep your home looking perfect all the time.
- You might not want to go to an event.
- You might sometimes let your politeness slip.

If you have made mistakes, were they met with compassion and understanding? Or was it all about perfection? The weight of those mistakes can feel unbearable, because you've been conditioned to believe that failure, or anything other than perfection, isn't an option. It steals your confidence, making you question your value, and keeps you trapped in a cycle of striving to meet impossible standards. However, your worth cannot be measured by your weight, your complexion or your ability to fit into a narrow set of behaviours. You are always enough, and the standards are the problem, not you.

In many households, parents feel their success is measured by their children's accomplishments, and a daughter's marriage is often seen as their crowning achievement. If you're not married by a certain age, the murmurs start: 'What's wrong with her?' Families feel the pressure of those words and, unfortunately, they pass that pressure on to you, but the fear of their daughters *not* getting married is real for them. Maybe you've felt it yourself, or maybe you've seen it happen to someone else in your community. The older you get, the louder the questions become: 'Why isn't she married yet?' And those questions aren't just annoying; they're invasive and deeply personal.

Being unmarried in South Asian culture often feels like you're being examined under a magnifying glass. People assume there must be something wrong with you. *Is she too picky? Does she have a bad attitude? Is she hiding something?* They don't judge boys in the same way. They don't think about other possibilities. They just think something is wrong with you. Your achievements, your kindness and everything else you bring to the table are suddenly irrelevant, just because you haven't ticked this one box.

When it's everyone's day but yours

For many Brown girls, particularly those who feel suffocated at home, marriage is sold as a ticket to freedom, and they choose it as a way to escape the family. Some achieve this, but for others it doesn't turn out the way they envisaged it. That's because marriage is never just a union between two people; it's a merging of two families.

The wedding isn't just about you and your partner. It's about parents, other relatives and sometimes even the neighbours. This idea of marriage as a family affair can raise a sense of belonging. When you marry into a South Asian family, you're often welcomed with open arms and surrounded by people who want to love and care for you. It can bring the following with it:

- **Support systems:** If you're lucky, you might gain in-laws who treat you with love, and who are there for you in times of joy and sorrow. Whether it's financial support, childcare or simply a shoulder to lean on, the extended family can be a pillar of strength.
- **Rich traditions:** The involvement of family means weddings are vibrant, elaborate celebrations filled with rituals that have been passed down for generations. These traditions can connect you to your roots and make you feel like part of something bigger.
- **Collective joy:** The idea of 'us' over 'me' can create a sense of unity. When done in a balanced way, families coming together can feel like a beautiful collaboration where everyone contributes to the happiness of the couple.

On the surface, this can all feel warm and celebratory, but beneath that warmth can lie a whole set of obligations and the potential loss of what it is you want. This means you can be left feeling torn between cultural expectations and your need for autonomy.

Handling proposals

Some of you may receive no proposals, resulting in society judging you and your confidence being impacted. Some of you may resent your parents for not looking, and some of you may resent your parents for the type of proposals they bring, tying them to your worth and making you wonder, *Is this what my parents think I'm worthy of?*

Some of you, on the other hand, may have had multiple proposals come your way and will know how exhausting the process of getting to know potential grooms can be, particularly because every time you get to know a person, someone always chips in with an opinion. Whether it's your auntie saying, 'No, he isn't good for her' or your mum saying, 'I don't like where they're from back home,' people have their opinions – and they give them freely. Meanwhile, no one thinks about how tedious and tiring this process is for you. You may have been sold a dream, but no one tells you how much of yourself you might have to give up to make that dream come true.

Even before you've confirmed if this proposal is what you truly want, people are staking claims on your time, your plans and your emotions, along with all their opinions, which can take away mental space for you to think clearly. For example, they may share their views on the proposal, how great or not this person is or what they want you to do. Sometimes, the wedding talk can begin happening at this early stage, too, which can add pressure. And there you are, hesitating, trying to figure out how to respond to the proposal.

The discussions around marriage start with how things *should* look: the hosting, the introductions, the endless opinions on how every day of the week-long event of the wedding needs to unfold. Somehow, it's hardly ever about you or what you want; it's about everyone else. From the moment the proposal happens, it's no longer just your moment. Who was invited to the proposal? Who wasn't? Who feels left out? Who wants to feel the most important? It's exhausting, and the proposal hasn't even been finalised yet.

In our culture, there's this fear of the *evil eye* – the idea that not everyone will want the best for you – so we're told to keep things minimal and to share as little as possible. But even then, the judgements come pouring in. If you've ever felt terrible for wanting to hold on to a little bit of privacy, let me tell you right now: that's not your fault. It's okay to want some things just for yourself, even if others don't understand it.

Wedding planning

And then comes the wedding planning itself. This is where it becomes clear that it's impossible to make everyone happy. You might want to choose specific colours for your bridal party, but someone will feel left out because they weren't asked for their opinion. You might share plans with a few close people, only to hear complaints from others who feel excluded. You'll find yourself agonising over decisions and carrying guilt for things that are beyond your control. The truth is, no matter how much you try, someone will always be upset. There will always be someone who says, 'Why didn't you think of me?' or 'I can't believe you hid this from me.' And in the midst of all this chaos, you start to feel yourself disappearing.

South Asian weddings, as beautiful as they are, often stop being about the bride and groom entirely. The focus shifts to the family, the community and the image they want to protect. Maybe you've heard things like, 'Why are you choosing to wear that?', 'It's too plain' or 'It's too much', or 'How will it look if we don't invite so-and-so?' It's like everyone gets a say except you, and you're expected to smile through it all. You may be struggling financially, yet that might not be considered. If you feel overwhelmed, resentful or just plain exhausted, I get it, because at the end of the day this is *your* moment, even if the world around you doesn't let it feel that way. I wish the people around you would simply say, 'We're happy if you're happy, because this is your day', but until they do, I hope you find the strength to say it to yourself. You deserve that.

You married the family

Talking about in-laws and marriage can feel incredibly heavy, and many of you will relate to what I'm about to share. For some, navigating in-law relationships has been an uphill battle, filled with tension, misunderstanding and emotional strain. For others, these relationships may be harmonious and supportive. The truth is, it often comes down to boundaries: knowing when to step in, when to step back and when to simply let things be. But the thing is, boundaries can feel pointless if you're outnumbered. When it's not just one person but an entire family dynamic you're up against, holding your ground can feel impossible.

For every touching story about supportive in-laws, there's a counter-narrative about families who overstep boundaries, impose their values and make the marriage about their needs instead of yours. Here are some examples of what commonly occurs in South Asian families:

- **Loss of privacy:** When families are deeply involved, it can feel like you're constantly being watched. Decisions that should be private, like how you and your partner manage your finances, where you live or how you raise children, are often publicly discussed among the family. They control what you do with your husband, where you go out … and the list goes on.
- **Expectations overload:** Pleasing your in-laws can feel like a full-time job. There might be unspoken (or spoken) rules about how you should dress, what you should cook and even how you address them. Over time, this can feel suffocating, as if you're losing parts of yourself to fit into their mould.
- **Pressure to 'perform':** When you marry into a family, you might feel the weight of representing your own family. If something goes wrong, if you don't perform to standards or meet expectations – perhaps you don't speak in a certain way or don't know how to cook a certain dish – it can feel like a reflection on your parents and your upbringing. That's because your husband's family might be quick to say, 'Haven't your parents taught you well' to shame you.

LIVING WITH YOUR IN-LAWS

There's a common saying: 'You're not just marrying the person, you're marrying their family.' For many South Asian women, marriage means living with the in-laws, often in a joint family situation. This can blur the lines between family life and the individual, and it can sometimes feel quite overwhelming. You're expected to juggle the dynamics of your partner's family while maintaining your relationship with your own family.

One of the hardest parts of marrying into another family is the implicit expectation that you should instantly know how they do things. The assumption is that because you share the same culture, you'll automatically understand their household norms. But what many fail to realise is that no two families are the same; every household has its own ways, values and unspoken rules.

Some families let go of some of the traditions; some families hold on to them. Maybe your in-laws believe in traditional gender roles, but you and your partner value something different. Or perhaps your own family expects you to 'win over' your in-laws, even if they're difficult. This can leave you feeling like you're the one making all the adjustments while still being judged or criticised for not getting it right.

It makes sense that the lessons you learned under your parents' roof – the silence, the sacrifice, the constant fear of disappointing others – are now shaping your relationships with your in-laws or your husband. They creep into your role as a wife, as a daughter-in-law, because those beliefs don't just disappear. You don't wake up one day and forget what it felt like to tiptoe around everyone's expectations. The questions still haunt you: *What will they think? Am I pleasing them? Am I good enough?* You've been prepared to serve for so long that it probably feels like second nature, even when it suffocates you.

And what about emotional connection? That absence you grew up with, does it echo now in your marriage? If no one asked what would make you happy back then, is anyone asking now? Or do you still feel invisible, like your voice doesn't matter? Maybe your in-laws have taken control in ways that feel creepily familiar. Perhaps they dismiss you, disregard you, treat you as an extension of their authority rather than as a person. And if they can't control you directly, maybe they do it through their son.

IMPACT ON YOUR MARRIAGE

It doesn't stop, does it? For many of you, marriage probably feels like a delicate balancing act. You want to honour your own family while building a relationship with your partner's family. But what happens when these two worlds collide? If you're too close to your own family, your in-laws might feel threatened. They might mutter things like, 'She's always at her mum's house.' But if you're too close to your in-laws, your own parents might feel abandoned, murmuring things like, 'Look, she's forgetting about us.'

In the middle of it all, you're trying to hold on to a relationship with your partner, which can feel like it's taking a back seat. This happens so often when you're juggling both families. Meanwhile, it's you two who got married, and you need to be able to make time for each other, but all the other responsibilities and expectations take over. Many in-laws fail to understand this, because for them there isn't an issue: you married the family, remember?

The part that hurts the most is that, once upon a time, there was a girl who believed this was her escape, her freedom ticket, her happily ever after. And now you're sitting here, suffocated, asking yourself, *Was my life always just about serving others?* That pain, the betrayal you feel, makes perfect sense. If you feel like you've been lied to, trapped in a story that wasn't yours to begin with, questioning whether anyone ever truly cared about *you*, I promise you: that pain is valid.

I am so deeply sorry for how much you were made to believe that marriage was your freedom, only to find yourself in the same chains. Parents genuinely believe they're looking out for you, offering wisdom and guidance, but love and tradition can sometimes blur into intrusion and control. The challenge lies in finding balance. How do you honour your family's values without losing yourself? How do you show respect without compromising your boundaries?

Marriage as a family affair can be beautiful, but it should never come at the cost of your happiness or identity. You're not ungrateful or selfish for wanting space to grow into your own role as a partner. You have a right to set gentle boundaries, to speak your truth and to build a relationship that feels authentic to you and your partner. Remember, the best families are the ones that allow you to be fully yourself, not just the version of you that they expect.

I see you. I see the weight you're carrying. And I want you to know that this narrative, this pressure, isn't your fault. It's a system that was built long before you were born, designed to keep women in a particular role. But you are not a role; you're a whole person. The truth is, your life doesn't begin or end with marriage. Marriage can be a beautiful part of your journey if you choose it, but it's not the only path to happiness, success or fulfilment. You are so much more than someone's current or future wife.

Women need protecting

There's an accepted truth in many South Asian communities: women need to be protected, shielded and provided for. The narrative has always been that a woman should never need to worry about finances, security or even a roof over her head, because that's a man's job. Until you marry, it's your father's job, and once you're married, it becomes your husband's job. This idea is deeply ingrained, and for generations it has shaped how families and societies approach a woman's purpose and value. However, to enable your husband to do his job properly, there are some unspoken rules of marriage you must follow:

- Be a 'good wife' by prioritising your husband and his family over yourself.
- Don't voice your disagreements too strongly, because it's your job to keep the peace.
- Don't be too opinionated; just nod your head.
- Don't ask for too much, don't be too much and don't speak too much about your emotions.
- Sacrifice your comfort, career or dreams if that's what it takes to make the marriage work.

While this protection can be an amazing thing to have – and many of you may deeply desire it – unfortunately, many husbands confuse the need to protect with control. As a result, the 'partnership' you were promised may not feel very equal. You were told that if you stayed patient, loyal and obedient, things would eventually fall into place; however, even when your husband didn't hold up his end of the bargain – whether by avoiding his responsibilities, failing to provide for you materially or not showing basic respect – you were still expected to carry on with yours. You were told to keep trying, to be understanding, to wait, because that's what a 'good wife' does.

Yes, as a wife, you might be encouraged to study, to focus on your career and to explore opportunities, but these are often framed as secondary interests. They aren't celebrated as milestones or achievements in the same way that marriage is. A career is nice to have, but marriage? Marriage is the ultimate goal, the ultimate achievement that truly defines a woman's worth. So, by being told your father and then your husband would look after you, you learned that even if you had a job, you didn't have to take it seriously because the men in your life would provide for you. This is a very limiting belief that creates many potential threats, such as the following:

- Lack of financial literacy
- Risk of financial abuse in a marriage

- Risk of a controlling partner
- Unable to leave an abusive toxic marriage due to financial dependency

There's a video I created and posted on TikTok (see link in the Resources section) in which I shared the following words. It touched thousands of hearts and resonated for many Brown girls, and if it resonates for you, too, I see you:

'As a South Asian girl it was instilled in many of us that when you are young, your father looks after you and then it's your husband. What life didn't prep many of us for is what happens when things don't go that way? What happens if it's not the way you believed it would be with so much conviction? What happens to the young girls who have an absent father? Single mothers? The women who went through divorce? . . . Nah, scrap that. What happens to women who just want to live?

'Isn't knowing how to live day to day a life skill? When it came to budgeting and finance I remember how overwhelming and anxiety-provoking it was. I felt embarrassed thinking, Fahima, you should know this, but how? How was I to know something that wasn't given any importance?

'So teach your girls how to use their voice, not just to nod their head. Don't just invest in her wedding, but teach her about finance and don't tell her that she doesn't have to worry about money. Teach her to feel self-sufficient, so everything else that comes her way is like added value. Prepare her for this big world outside your home, because not every girl and woman will share the same scripted narrative you may want.'

Menstruation and intimacy

Talking about menstruation has long been a taboo, especially in Brown cultures, making it one of the many unspoken realities of marriage. Yet it's impossible to talk about marriage without addressing it. Far too many Brown women enter marriage without truly understanding their own bodies, let alone intimacy. They haven't been taught how their menstrual cycle affects their mood, energy and needs. They've never been given the space to talk about their own desires or to learn what healthy intimacy actually looks like. Instead, they're expected to simply 'know', as though it's instinctive – and if they don't, they're made to feel ashamed for it.

The menstrual cycle itself is a natural process, but many women have little knowledge of its different stages. During menstruation, the body sheds its uterine lining, often leaving women tired, achy or emotionally low. In the follicular phase, energy levels rise and women may feel more motivated or creative. Ovulation, the peak of fertility, often brings a natural boost in mood and a desire for intimacy. The luteal phase, which leads into menstruation, can bring irritability, anxiety or fatigue.

These shifts are completely normal, but without understanding them, women may feel confused or blame themselves for changes in their mood and energy. It also means their partners may be unaware of how to be sensitive or supportive.

When it comes to intimacy, many women are raised to see it as something they 'give' to their husbands rather than a shared experience. Their own needs and desires are often ignored or dismissed. This is not only unfair; it's untrue. Women, just like men, have emotional and physical needs. Intimacy should be about connection, comfort and pleasure for both partners. Yet many women feel ashamed for expressing their own desires or struggle to communicate their needs.

Worse still, the lack of education around intimacy leaves women vulnerable. I've heard far too many stories of coercion in marriage, where women feel pressured into intercourse they do not want. In some cases, they are even subjected to marital rape, which is tragically dismissed under the excuse of 'marital rights'. Educating women about their menstrual health, emotional needs and right to pleasure and boundaries isn't just empowering; it's necessary. When women are kept in the dark about their own bodies and their right to consent, they are left powerless, and that can have many impacts:

- **Lack of body awareness:** Many women grow up disconnected from their own bodies, unaware of how their menstrual cycle affects their emotions and well-being.
- **Neglected needs in marriage:** Intimacy is often treated as a duty rather than a shared experience, leaving women's needs unmet.
- **Shame around desire:** Women are made to feel guilty or dirty for expressing their sexual needs or setting boundaries.
- **Power imbalance:** Lack of education makes women more vulnerable to coercion, manipulation and marital abuse.
- **Emotional and physical disconnect:** If they don't understand their bodies, women can feel distant from their own sexuality and struggle to communicate their needs.

- **Generational silence:** Taboos keep women uninformed, leaving the next generation just as unprepared.
- **Unfulfilling marriages:** When intimacy is based on obligation rather than connection, marriages can become emotionally strained.

Did you hear she got divorced?

Divorce is, and has always been, a huge stigma in the South Asian community. It's not just frowned upon; it's seen as a personal flaw, a failure, a shameful secret. Women learn that they need to make their marriages work whatever the cost, because divorce represents everything you mustn't do: disrespect your family, break a sacred bond or go against cultural norms. There are no ifs or buts – nothing else matters but staying in a marriage.

And it's always the woman who's expected to work at the marriage, never the man. When people comment that you 'couldn't hold down a marriage', they mean it was you who couldn't keep the family ties, who couldn't maintain the relationship with your in-laws, who wasn't patient with your husband, who couldn't stay quiet, be strong and keep enduring like the women before you did.

Divorce rates have certainly increased, even in the South Asian community, and many people still view this as a very negative thing, but that's not how I think about it. For me, it's not so clear-cut. When I hear about divorce rates going up, I reflect on the following:

- Finally, people are choosing themselves.
- Finally, people are coming out of unhappy lives.
- Finally, people are saying 'no' to financial, physical and emotional abuse.
- Finally, people are choosing not to suffer in silence.

I also reflect on how relationships are now presented on social media and the rise of 'couple goals' and 'perfect' unrealistic expectations. I reflect on the romanticised version of relationships this creates and the pressure this puts on individuals.

SITTING IN JUDGEMENT

Women stay in unhappy marriages out of fear or financial dependency, for the children, because they fear being alone or even because they feel like their marital home is slightly better than their family home, even if both are abusive.

But remember, the women who stay have often built up resentment towards their husbands and in-laws. They may be extremely unhappy but think it's too late to leave. And they are probably mothers, who then talk about their unfulfilled lives to their children or family; if they find their voice at all, it is only when their children grow older and most times then start to speak up on their behalf. These families could certainly be described as dysfunctional, and none of this is good for anyone's mental health.

Making a marriage work should not be at the expense of a woman (or indeed her children), but you have internalised the belief that you should:

- stay even if he's controlling you;
- stay even if he's physically abusing you;
- stay even if he's sexually assaulting you;
- stay even if you're unhappy, because no one else will look after you now;
- stay even if he has you as a prisoner in your own home;
- stay even if he and his family are treating you like a slave;
- stay because no one else will marry you;
- stay because you have to endure the same pain others had to face before you;
- stay even if your mental health is so poor you don't want to live anymore;
- stay because you are too frightened to leave in case of reprisals.

When a marriage ends, society sees it not just as a relationship that didn't work but as a failure on your part. The size of the failure matches the importance that marriage is given in the South Asian community, and a lot of criticism is likely to be doled out. Here are some of the more common attitudes divorced women experience:

- **You didn't try hard enough:** The narrative is always about what *you* could have done differently. Could you have been more patient, more understanding, more forgiving? Even in situations where the marriage is abusive or toxic, women are often told to adjust or give it another chance.

- **This family has a bad name because of you:** Divorce doesn't just impact you; it's often seen as a stain on your family's reputation. Questions like, 'What will people think of us?' or 'How will your siblings get married?' add layers of guilt and pressure to an already painful decision. You're made to feel that you've damaged the family's reputation.
- **The blame game:** In many cases, divorced women are labelled as difficult or too modern. The husband is rarely held to account, and the complexity of relationships is seldom acknowledged. Instead, the blame falls entirely on you. It's always the woman's fault.
- **The 'damaged goods' label:** Once divorced, women are often treated as if they're used or somehow less than. It's a deeply dehumanising perspective that makes you feel unworthy of love or happiness.
- **You won't get a second chance:** Unlike men, who are often encouraged to remarry quickly, divorced women are seen as a 'last resort' in the marriage market. You might hear people say things to prospective partners like, 'You could do better – why are you going for a divorcée?' Families tend to discourage proposals from or to divorced women, believing it reflects poorly on their social status. In fact, parents may say no purely on that basis.
- **Loss of community:** For many women, their marriage ties them to a specific social circle or community, or even family. Divorce can sever those ties, leaving you to rebuild your life with little or no support, especially if the family told you to stay and you didn't listen to them. This fear of being alone, emotionally, socially and even financially, can be used against you and keeps many women in marriages that feel more like a prison than a partnership.
- **Think of the children:** For mothers, the fear of divorce often revolves around how it will affect their kids. You might be told things like, 'They need both parents', 'A broken home will ruin their future' and 'How will you get them married?' Of course, the threat of damaging your children is very powerful; however, while it's true that divorce can be challenging for children, having parents who stay in an unhealthy marriage can be even more damaging for them.
- **You will harm your parents:** Similarly, no one wants to feel that they could cause their parents stress or, even worse,

precipitate health issues for them, but the community can be very judgemental if it thinks that by getting divorced you're not giving due consideration to your elders.
- **The fantasy of harmony:** Other people might tell you that keeping your marriage intact is better than dealing with the fallout. You might even tell yourself that, but pretending everything is fine comes at the cost of your mental health, your sense of self and your happiness.

As I've said, women are taught to keep their struggles private, to endure in silence and to never let the cracks show. This culture of secrecy creates a cycle of shame and isolation, making it harder for women to seek help or support. Marriage is meant to be a beautiful thing, so why should it feel like a life sentence? If a relationship no longer aligns with your well-being, you deserve the freedom to choose a different path, without shame, without fear and without judgement.

Dismantling The Traditional Narrative

For so many of us, marriage was handed to us as a pre-packaged ideal. It wasn't a choice; it was a destiny, an expectation, a rite of passage into adulthood. But what if we could take that package, unwrap it and decide for ourselves what it means to us? What if marriage wasn't about ticking boxes or living up to someone else's standards, but about creating a bond that aligns with your values, your dreams and your truth?

As we begin dismantling the traditional beliefs around marriage, I invite you to give yourself permission to see marriage differently. Begin to rewrite the story so that marriage is no longer a duty or a finish line but a partnership built on respect, understanding and love.

Arranged marriages and forced marriages

I began this chapter with a reference to arranged marriage in *Bridgerton*, and I want to start this section by picking that up. We all know the difference between an arranged marriage and a forced marriage, right?

Arranged marriage, at its best, can be a beautiful process of collaboration, mutual respect and safety. It's about families coming together, genuinely listening to each other and trusting the decisions made not just by them but also by *you*. There's space for your voice, your needs and your future in those conversations, and it feels like a team effort, where everyone is working towards your happiness.

That sense of support can feel incredibly reassuring, especially because if young girls use online apps (as many do these days), there can be a lot of risks of catfishing, predators, grooming and so on. Hence, many young women prefer their families to bring proposals to them, because they trust their loved ones to safeguard them.

But then there's coercion, and that's where the lines blur. Coercion doesn't always look like someone physically forcing you into a marriage. Sometimes, it's much quieter, much harder to detect, but just as damaging. It's the manipulation, the subtle or not-so-subtle guilt trips, the way the family frames their desires as if they're yours. It's the countless ways in which they make you feel like you don't have a choice without ever explicitly saying, 'You have no choice.'

Think about it: if you grew up in a household where your voice was never valued, where thinking for yourself wasn't encouraged or where decisions were always made for you, how would you even know how to advocate for yourself? In those moments, others aren't talking *with* you; they're talking *at* you – and your consent, your ability to freely say 'yes' or 'no', is quietly stolen.

For example, imagine you're told, 'You know how much we've done for you – this marriage will make us happy', or 'Look, everyone's saying he's great', or maybe it's 'You're getting older and good proposals don't come often. Do you want to end up alone?' Statements like these are loaded with guilt, fear and manipulation. They don't give you room to decide what you truly want, and they carefully construct a cage that makes you feel like agreeing is your only option.

This is coercion. It's being pressured, guilt tripped or manipulated into a marriage. It chips away at your ability to think for yourself until you feel you have no choice but to comply. That's the painful reality for many women, but understand this: when your voice isn't truly heard, when your thoughts and feelings aren't given the space they deserve, your consent isn't real.

Coercion is when:

- your parents put enormous effort into convincing you a proposal is great for you;
- everyone around you pretends to be super-happy about the match, which is out of character and creates doubt in your mind;
- your feelings and concerns are dismissed;
- they insist you won't find 'better' or make you feel you're not worthy of 'better';
- you're pressurised to make a decision quickly or they will make it for you.

Pause, assess, proceed

Marriage is a very important life decision and no one can – or should – rush you into it. This three-step framework is perfect for navigating any high-pressure situation. It gives you permission to slow down and take your time, and it's a simple but incredibly effective way of taking back control of decisions.

If your thoughts are clouded, just pause, even if others are in a rush around you. Find a noise-free place where you can sort out what your viewpoint is or speak to a someone who can help you think more clearly:

1. **Pause:** When you feel overwhelmed by pressure or guilt, take a moment to breathe. Remind yourself: *I am not obliged to make a decision right now.*
2. **Assess:** Ask yourself questions like: *Do I feel rushed? Do I have all the information I need about this person and situation? Does this decision align with my values and long-term happiness?*
3. **Proceed:** Only move forward when you feel you have clarity and peace about your decision, not because others are pushing you.

In the traditional narrative, marriage often feels like something you *have to do*. The timelines are set, the expectations are clear and the pressure to conform can be overwhelming. But redefining marriage means seeing it as a choice, not a duty – and when you see marriage as a choice, it gives you the power to walk away if it doesn't feel right (*see the box on p. 115 for a more detailed exploration*). It allows you to say, 'I deserve a partnership that feels fulfilling, not just one that looks good to others.'

> ### Remember, you can always say 'no'
>
> Never be trapped into accepting a marriage proposal that you don't want to accept. Don't be manipulated into saying 'yes', and don't allow others to bully you into saying 'yes'. Some people will want you to say 'yes' because you and probably both families have invested time and effort into the process. But if you hadn't done that, how would you have known whether to say 'yes' or 'no'? It's a momentous decision, and there's no rush.
>
> You may have heard of people calling off a wedding at a late stage. This may even have been you. Of course, no one wants to do that, but sometimes something just doesn't feel right. So, listen to your gut instead of thinking, *What will people say?* If you do have to call off a wedding, know that it is an act of self-love and bravery. I repeat: it is okay to take time when you're making a life decision, because you want to make the right decision for yourself, for your potential husband and for both your families. A gentle reminder: it's about marrying well, not marrying quickly.

Understanding what coercion looks like is important, but it's just one side of the coin. Let's turn our attention to something more positive: how to recognise when you're in a healthy relationship.

What healthy relationships look like

As a therapist, I've found time and time again that people can't describe what a healthy relationship looks like – and how do you achieve a healthy relationship if you don't have a model? I know that as children, many of you may not have had the opportunity to observe healthy relationships for yourselves, so I want to walk through some of the elements with you:

- **Emotional intelligence**
    - **Self-awareness:** Both partners can recognise and express their emotions clearly without fear or defensiveness.
    - **Empathy:** You strive to understand each other's feelings, even when you don't agree.
    - **Regulation:** Instead of reacting impulsively during conflicts, you pause, process their emotions and respond thoughtfully.
    - ***Reflection prompt:*** *How do I feel when my partner listens to me during emotional moments?*

- **Maturity**
  - **Accountability:** Both partners take responsibility for their actions instead of blaming the other.
  - **Perspective:** You understand that challenges are a part of life and approach them as a team.
  - **Patience:** You don't rush decisions or expect perfection, but allow room for growth.
  - *Reflection prompt:* Does my partner handle conflict in a way that prioritises resolution and mutual respect, or is it just about who's right and who's wrong?

- **Open communication**
  - **Honesty:** Partners are transparent about their feelings, thoughts and needs without fear of judgement.
  - **Active listening:** You truly hear each other, without interrupting or dismissing.
  - **Non-defensiveness:** Feedback is received as an opportunity for growth, not as a personal attack.
  - *Reflection prompt:* Can we talk openly about our concerns without it escalating into conflict? (Conflicts are normal; what's important is how you both work on coming back together in harmony.)

- **Mutual respect**
  - **Boundaries:** Each partner respects the other's physical, emotional and mental boundaries, and also their family boundaries – you can love and respect each other's families while still maintaining boundaries.
  - **Relationship prioritisation:** A healthy marriage allows you to put yourselves first without guilt or pressure to over-compromise.
  - **Appreciation:** You both feel valued and seen for who you are, not just for what you do.
  - *Reflection prompt:* Do I feel respected in my individuality or am I expected to meet someone else's expectations?

- **Emotional and physical safety**
  - **Trust:** Neither partner manipulates, deceives or uses guilt as a tool for control.

- **Support:** You both provide a safe space for the other, where you can share vulnerabilities without fear of ridicule.
- **Physical boundaries:** You prioritise consent and comfort in all physical interactions.
- *Reflection prompt:* *Do I feel safe expressing my true self in this relationship?*

- **Shared goals and values**
  - **Future vision:** Both partners align on the big life decisions (family, finances, lifestyle).
  - **Core beliefs:** You respect each other's values while also having overlapping ones that guide the relationship.
  - **Fluidity:** You can adapt when life doesn't go as planned while still staying connected.
  - *Reflection prompt:* *Do we share a similar vision for the future, and can we adapt when things change?*

- **Growth-oriented mindset**
  - **Adaptability:** Both partners are open to personal and relational growth.
  - **Curiosity:** You seek to learn more about yourselves and each other, even years into the relationship.
  - **Encouragement:** You celebrate each other's growth instead of feeling threatened by it.
  - *Reflection prompt:* *Does my partner encourage me to grow, or does he hold me back out of fear, insecurity or control?*

- **Healthy conflict resolution**
  - **Fairness:** You avoid bringing up old wounds or using the silent treatment.
  - **Problem-solving:** You focus on resolving the issue rather than winning the argument.
  - **Reconnection:** After a disagreement, you make an effort to reconnect and heal.
  - *Reflection prompt:* *Do we work through conflicts in a way that strengthens the relationship rather than weakens it?*

- **Emotional connection**
  - **Validation:** Each person feels heard, seen, understood and valued in their emotions.
  - **Vulnerability:** You are able to share fears, dreams and struggles without fear of judgement.
  - **Consistency:** Emotional connection is nurtured regularly, not just during difficult times.
  - **Reflection prompt:** *Do I feel emotionally connected to my partner, or do I feel alone even when we're together? Are we just existing and playing the roles?*

- **Fun, playfulness and friendship**
  - **Laughter:** You make time to enjoy each other's company and create happy memories.
  - **Companionship:** You share interests and genuinely enjoy spending time together.
  - **Positivity:** You focus on appreciating the good in each other, even when things are hard.
  - **Reflection prompt:** *Is there joy and lightness in our relationship, or does it feel like all work and no play?*

- **Independence within togetherness**
  - **Individual identity:** Both partners maintain their own hobbies, friendships and passions.
  - **No co-dependence:** You rely on each other for support, but are not overly dependent for happiness or fulfilment on your partner. One person cannot be your everything at all times, so it's good to have a wider support system, too.
  - **Encouraging autonomy:** You cheer each other on in your personal goals.
  - **Reflection prompt:** *Do we encourage each other to grow as individuals while staying connected as a couple?*

This next exercise will help you understand your own expectations of your relationship and how this compares to the reality.

Exercise: Reflections on a healthy relationship 🧩

On the previous page, I listed the aspects of healthy relationships that I believe are important, so let's now look at an exercise to reflect on this:

1. **Reflect individually:** Take some quiet time on your own. Write down what a *healthy relationship* looks like to you. Be honest and specific – think about how you want to feel, how conflict is handled, how love is shown and what safety and respect mean to you.
2. **Invite your partner:** Ask your partner to do the same exercise separately. No peeking or discussing until you're both done.
3. **Share and compare:** Come together and share what you each wrote. Notice the similarities – these can become your shared values. Pay attention to the differences too – they're not necessarily problems but rather opportunities to understand each other more deeply.
4. **Reflect together:** Use this conversation to explore where you align, where you differ and how you can work together to create a relationship that feels healthy and safe for both of you. You may not agree on everything, and that's okay – the goal isn't perfection but mutual understanding and growth.

Everyone has their own definitions and there may be some things that you don't agree on, because people are different and every relationship is different. However, the point of this exercise is for you to know what you see as healthy and what your partner sees as healthy, and how you can work together to achieve that.

It's not about other couples, your parents' relationship or what you see on social media; it's about what you both want in your relationship. So, even if your list of the features of healthy relationships is very different from mine, you're allowed to take what you need and leave what you don't. An important reminder here is that it's still healthy if you're working towards each of the things you listed that you want; it becomes unhealthy when someone chooses to remain the same and not to work on things that are unhealthy, even though it's impacting the other person.

MATURE LOVE

A central element of healthy relationships is mature love, which is rooted in openness, not in power or control. It's not about shaping you into someone else's idea of who you should be or forcing you to fit into a mould they find comfortable. It allows you to bring all versions of yourself, including those that might be messy, imperfect or still figuring things out. In mature love, there's space to stumble and make mistakes without the fear of being abandoned or judged.

True connection means both people can exist fully as they are, growing together and seeing that growth unfold. It's not about one person overshadowing the other or one person making all the sacrifices. It's a partnership where both lives are honoured and where there's space for both voices, both perspectives and both sets of needs.

Mature love doesn't just celebrate the parts of you that are easy to love; it accepts the parts that are challenging, the ones that don't always shine. It doesn't ask you to pretend, to suppress your emotions or to shrink yourself just to maintain peace. Instead, it encourages growth, honesty and vulnerability.

This kind of love makes room for complexity. It's not a rigid structure where every role is predefined but a fluid, evolving space where both people can change and grow, together and individually. It nurtures a connection where being real is more important than being perfect. It allows patience, it allows leaning on one another and it understands you're both trying your best – and that's good enough.

Love itself is not enough if it's not paired with mutual respect, understanding and freedom, because love without these elements can become a cage: something that binds rather than liberates. Mature love, on the other hand, is about liberation. It's about building a life where two people can stand side by side, with all their flaws and beauty intact.

In South Asian culture, we're often fed the idea of a 'perfect' marriage. The husband is successful and loving, the wife is devoted and nurturing and the family lives in harmony. But life isn't a Bollywood movie, and real marriages are messy, complex and far from perfect.

Maybe you and your partner don't fit into traditional gender roles and you're both okay with that. Maybe you live in separate cities for work, or maybe you argue sometimes and have to work through it. None of that makes your marriage less valid, and we should let go of the idea that marriage – or your wedding – has to look a certain way.

The wedding tug of war

Dismantling the overwhelming expectations surrounding South Asian weddings isn't easy, but it's possible to navigate them gently and in a way that feels respectful to others while still honouring yourself. Many of the behaviours and demands you'll face are deeply rooted in cultural traditions, family dynamics and even fear. Understanding why others behave the way they do can help you approach these situations with empathy while setting boundaries that prioritise your well-being. So, why does everyone else have all these opinions?

- **Cultural norms and shared responsibility:** Weddings are often seen as a family milestone, not just a personal one. Families believe they're upholding traditions and taking collective responsibility for ensuring everything's done right. For them, your wedding reflects the family's status, unity and values. To them, it's not just about you; it's about the togetherness.
- **Fear of judgement:** Your parents and relatives may genuinely fear being judged by the community. Statements like 'What will people say?' often come from a place of vulnerability, where people feel their reputation and self-worth are tied to how well the wedding meets expectations. The auntie you've never heard of needs to be invited because she'll be upset if she's not. It's a lot about people-pleasing.
- **Desire to feel included:** Many relatives feel a deep attachment to family events and want to be involved. When they push to be part of the process or express disappointment, it's often because they want to feel valued and connected, not because they want to upset you. Yes, it's hard to make sense of it, yet it's about togetherness over individuality.

You might even feel annoyed, thinking, *Some of you have had your day – you've been the bride already – so why don't you just let me have mine?* I get it, and it's valid, but I'm going to share how you can gently navigate this situation...

HANDLING WEDDING PLANS WITH TACT

At the end of the day, navigating a South Asian wedding isn't about winning a battle against expectations; it's about finding balance. You deserve to have a wedding that reflects your values and brings you joy while also honouring the relationships that matter to you. Start small, stay firm on what's most important and know that it's okay to prioritise yourself in a process that so often asks you to prioritise everyone else:

- **Start with open communication**
    - Have honest conversations with your parents or key family members early on. Let them know what's most important to you and why.
    - For example, use language that emphasises collaboration, like 'I know this is a big moment for all of us, and I really want us to plan something that feels special while also keeping some things simple for my own peace of mind' or 'I value your opinions and guidance, but I also need space to make certain decisions that feel right for me.'

- **Set clear boundaries with compassion**
    - Decide early on what you're willing to compromise on and what's non-negotiable for you.
    - For example, if you want to keep your engagement details private for now, explain gently, 'I know everyone's excited, but I'd like to keep this between us until I feel ready to share it more widely as it helps me process everything better.'

- **Redirect the focus**
    - When relatives make the event about themselves, acknowledge their feelings but redirect the focus back to what's important to you.
    - For example, 'I understand that you want to be involved and I truly appreciate your support, so I will let you know when I need some help.'

- **Lean on a trusted support system**
    - Identify a sibling, cousin or friend who can act as a mediator or buffer when emotions run high. They can help you navigate conflicts with relatives while you focus on enjoying the process. This really helps take the attention off you, so you aren't soaking up all the emotions that are being projected.

- **Be strategic about sharing information**
  - Instead of sharing every detail with everyone, limit updates to a smaller circle of people you trust. This reduces the number of opinions and unnecessary feedback.

- **Recognise when it's not about you**
  - When someone's upset over colour themes or guest lists, remind yourself that it's often more about their expectations or emotions than it is about you. It's okay to let those moments pass without internalising them.

I know it can be frustrating, but sometimes it helps to reframe things. Traditions don't have to feel burdening, so choose the ones you like and enjoy and respectfully leave the ones you don't. Ultimately, ask yourself, *What matters most right now?* Because when this phase passes, what won't matter is whether you met every single expectation. I want to remind you that many of the demands come from love and a desire to see you happy. Yes, it can feel hard to see that at the time, especially if it's expressed in ways that don't always align with what you want, but recognising this can help you approach the process with more patience and grace.

Respecting our elders in a healthy way is all about building understanding and finding a balance that works for both sides. It's great to appreciate the wisdom and experiences they bring, and it's just as important to honour your own individuality and the choices you want to make for your life. It can be helpful to think about where cultural expectations might have blurred those important boundaries and gently challenge them when needed. If certain demands feel a bit too much, it's perfectly okay to push back respectfully by saying something like, 'It would mean a lot to me if you could trust me to make this decision.'

Navigating this dynamic doesn't mean disrespecting elders or disregarding their experiences. It means challenging the entitlement that comes at the expense of your boundaries and well-being. It means redefining respect to include mutual understanding, accountability and dialogue. Here are some ways to approach this gently yet assertively:

- **Redefine respect:** Respect doesn't mean submission; it means valuing someone's perspective while maintaining your ability to express your own.

- **Set clear boundaries:** Politely but firmly communicate your limits. For example, 'I value your input, but I need to learn to make this decision on my own.'
- **Acknowledge their intentions:** Often, entitlement stems from a place of care or fear for you. Acknowledge their concerns, but also share your needs. For example, 'I understand you want the best for me, but I also need space to figure out what's right for me.'
- **Seek allies:** Sometimes, having a supportive family member or friend who understands both sides can help bridge the gap.
- **Let go of guilt:** Recognise that setting boundaries isn't disrespectful but self-preservation. You can honour your elders without sacrificing yourself.

This is all about balance. It's about creating space for both the respect you've been taught to show and the boundaries you deserve to have. Elders may have lived longer, but that doesn't mean their experiences invalidate your own. Respect isn't a weapon; it's a bridge. And it's okay to ask for that bridge to go both ways.

Ditching the perfect wife image

In traditional narratives, marriage can feel like a performance. You've seen mothers, quite possibly your own mother, play a role, but your marriage shouldn't be about how it looks to others – it should be about how it feels to you. When you strip away the performance, marriage becomes a partnership. It's about building a life that feels fulfilling for both you and your partner.

First of all, you're enough just as you are – your skin, your body, your voice, your dreams. The messages telling you your worth is tied to your appearance or your performance of the role of 'wife' and 'mother' are horrible, because they make you doubt yourself at every turn. So, let's take a step back. The idea of perfection is a lie. No one, no matter how beautiful or accomplished they are, is perfect. The real question is, *Why should you have to be perfect?*

The perfect bride narrative isn't entirely black and white. For many families, these teachings come from a place of love and a desire to protect you. They believe that by preparing you to be a good wife, they're setting you up for a stable, happy life.

But here's where the conflict lies: the world has changed, and so have you. The qualities that make a good partner today – empathy, communication and mutual respect – can't be boiled down to how well you make chai or how quietly you adjust to new situations.

If you find yourself struggling with the heaviness of the perfect bride ideal, know this: you don't have to reject all of it to reclaim your power. You can keep the values that resonate with you, like respect, grace or self-sufficiency, and let go of the ones that don't. Ask yourself the following questions:

- *Do these expectations serve or limit me?*
- *Am I striving for perfection or embracing authenticity?*
- *Do I want to live up to their standards or set my own?*

You are worthy not because of how well you cook, how gracefully you walk or how pleasing you are to others. You are worthy simply because you exist, and if you choose to step into a marriage, you deserve to do so as your full, authentic self.

Exercise: Reflections on being the perfect bride

This exercise will help you to gently uncover the rules you've been carrying about what it means to be a perfect bride. It's not about rejecting family, in-laws, or the joy of showing up for loved ones. It's about noticing the cost when your own needs, voice or identity are constantly pushed aside in order to be seen as 'good enough'. In South Asian cultures, acts of service and community care are beautiful, however when they come at the expense of your self-worth, self-abandonment, authenticity or mental health, it becomes necessary to pause. This tool creates that pause, a space to question what truly serves you, and what needs to be lovingly released.

- **Purpose:** Bring awareness to internalised cultural expectations.
- **Write down** everything you have ever been told (directly or indirectly) makes a 'good' or 'perfect' bride. For example: 'She should always be cooking', 'She should be slim', 'She should never raise her voice'.
- **Then ask yourself:** Do I agree with this? What would it cost me to keep living by this rule? Who does this serve? Can I find a balance with this if I do enjoy it but it now feels like a chore?

- **Why this helps:** This breaks the cycle of automatic compliance by helping women consciously question and reject inherited beliefs. Naming them reduces their power.

For many South Asian women, the pressure to look a certain way can feel suffocating. Who benefits when you hate your body? Society? Beauty industries? The answer is certainly not you. Loving your body isn't easy, especially if you grew up being shamed for it, but it starts with small acts of kindness towards yourself:

- **Challenge the inner critic:** When that voice in your head tells you you're not thin or fair enough, or you're too thin or not pretty enough, ask yourself: *Would I say this to a friend?* Treat yourself with the same kindness you'd show to someone you care about.
- **Surround yourself with positive messages:** Follow people on social media who celebrate diverse bodies and beauty standards. Seeing yourself represented can remind you that there's no one 'right' way to look.
- **Reconnect with your body:** Move, dance, rest, do things that make your body feel good – not because you want to change it, but because you want to honour it. Your body isn't a project or a problem to solve. It's the home you live in, and it deserves love and respect just as it is.

Another part of the perfect bride narrative is the expectation that you must speak in a certain way: softly, sweetly, never too loudly and certainly never in a way that challenges anyone. Maybe you've learned to bite your tongue because you've seen what happens to women who speak too much. Breaking free means letting go of the fear that speaking up makes you less desirable. It's okay to disagree. It's okay to have boundaries.

One of the most powerful ways to break free from the perfect bride narrative is to redefine beauty for yourself. Beauty isn't about matching a standard; it's about how you light up when you're talking about something you love, the way you show kindness to others and the unique qualities that make you *you*. You can take the first step with the 'Reflections on beauty' exercise on the next page.

Exercise: Reflections on beauty

If you grew up in an environment where a huge amount of importance was placed on appearance, you may have internalised this belief, and it may still consume your thoughts. Take some time to think about how you feel about outward appearances, and use the following prompts to see if you can shift those feelings:

- Think about the people in your life – is their appearance a factor in why you're close to them?
- What do you find beautiful in others that has nothing to do with their appearance?
- How do you feel about your appearance today?
- Which parts of yourself have you overlooked because you were focused on 'fixing' something else?
- What does beauty look like for you?
- What would happen if you chose to see yourself through a lens of love instead of judgement?
- What are the positives of accepting your appearance as it is?
- What are the negatives of accepting your appearance as it is?
- Outside your physical appearance, how else is your body serving you?

Say it with me: 'I am more than my looks. I am more than a bride. I am enough.' Take a deep breath and let go of the pressure to be perfect. It's okay to be real, to be flawed, to be human. In fact, that's where your true beauty lies.

Case study

Salma believes her skin colour has held her back

Salma, who is 28, Bangladeshi and a doctor, struggles with self-esteem and confidence. She has a darker complexion than her siblings, and growing up, she heard relatives frequently remark on her skin colour. They constantly made comments such as, 'Who will marry you?', 'You're the ugly duckling' and 'Don't go out in the sun or you'll get darker'. These made her feel unworthy and not deserving of love.

> When it was time to look for potential partners, she noticed descriptions from men and their families about what they were looking for in a bride, which said things like, 'Needs to be fair.' She told me, 'I want to believe that colourism does not exist today, but it does!'
>
> Salma struggles with her appearance, which she believes is why she's not married yet. So, I worked on separating her self-worth from her skin and explored her relationship with the mirror. The following affirmations were a gentle way to introduce self compassion:
>
> - I am beautiful in my skin, in my body and in all parts of me.
> - My brown skin is glowing and is a shade that's unique.
> - I am showing compassion to myself and embracing the colour of my skin.

Stopping the in-laws overload

As I discussed earlier (*see* pp. 102–5), in-laws often feel like an extension of your marriage. You don't just marry your partner; you marry their family, too. While that can come with warmth and support, it can also blur the lines between where your marriage ends and your in-laws begin. Setting gentle boundaries with your in-laws isn't about being disrespectful or distant but about protecting your space, your relationship and your peace of mind. When you grow up hearing all the horror stories about other women's experiences, it creates anxiety for a lot of women, which then bleeds into their relationships with their in-laws. So, let's talk about how you can navigate this delicate terrain.

You've probably grown up hearing that respecting your elders is non-negotiable. Of course, respect is important, but respect doesn't mean losing your independence or allowing others to dictate how you live your life. Respect is a two-way street. You can honour your in-laws' role in your family while also making sure they honour your autonomy.

For example, if your in-laws have opinions about how you run your household or live your life, it's okay to listen politely but still make your own decisions. You can say, 'Thank you for your advice; I'll think about that.' That response is respectful, but it also makes it clear that the final choice is yours. Similarly, if you feel overwhelmed by constant involvement, you can suggest a middle ground by saying something like, 'I'd love to have your input sometimes, but for day-to-day decisions I'd like to handle things myself, because it helps me grow.'

If you find yourself entering your in-laws' home as a newlywed, you need to give yourself a chance to get to know them. Between you and them, there's a huge blank space filled with ignorance, anxiety and fear – on both sides – and that leaves a lot of room for misunderstandings. Just be clear with yourself what your boundaries are.

You might feel pressure to put their comfort, preferences and needs above your own or even above your relationship, but a healthy marriage thrives when the couple puts each other first. Not in a selfish way, but in a way that builds a strong foundation for the whole family.

Imagine this scenario: your in-laws expect you and your partner to spend every weekend with them, but you feel it's cutting into your time together. Instead of ignoring your feelings, have an honest conversation with your partner. Say something like, 'I love spending time with your family, but I also think it's important for us to have some weekends to ourselves. Can we find a balance that works for both?' By prioritising your marriage, you're not neglecting your in-laws – you're ensuring that your relationship stays strong, which benefits everyone in the long run.

For so many of you, saying no feels like the ultimate disrespect. You've been taught to comply, to adjust, to go along with what's expected, but you are allowed to say 'no', even to your in-laws. I can understand why it's difficult to do so, but 'no' doesn't have to come from a place of anger or rebellion. It can come from a place of self-respect. For example, if they show up unannounced and it disrupts your plans, it's okay to say, 'We love having you over, but can we plan visits in advance next time?'

Boundaries often come with guilt, but guilt is a feeling, not a fact. You can acknowledge it without letting it control your actions. Over time, as you practise setting gentle boundaries, the guilt will lessen and you'll find you're more confident in standing up for yourself. You are not selfish or rude for setting limits. In fact, boundaries are an act of love, not just for yourself but for your relationship and for the family dynamic. They prevent resentment from building and create clarity about what's okay and what's not. You're teaching your in-laws about you so you can maintain these relationships.

Let's take a moment to think about why in-laws might struggle with boundaries. They might be coming from a place of love and concern, wanting to stay involved in your life, or they might be holding on to traditional expectations of what a daughter-in-law 'should' do. It's important to approach these situations with empathy and understanding, so while you have every right to set boundaries, doing so with kindness can make a world of difference. For example, instead of saying, 'Stop interfering in our marriage!', you can say, 'We really value your input, but we'd like to work on this ourselves.' Instead of pushing them away, invite them into your life in ways that feel comfortable for you: family dinners, shared celebrations or phone calls on your terms. After all, they want to be part of your life, too.

Boundaries don't have to create distance; they can create clarity. When everyone knows where they stand, relationships become healthier and more respectful. Even if it feels uncomfortable at first, you're allowed to prioritise your peace and you're allowed to define what family means to you.

It's possible to build a relationship with your in-laws that's rooted in mutual respect, not sacrifice. It's possible to love and honour them without losing yourself. And, most importantly, it's possible to create a life where you feel safe, valued and free. Take a look at the 'Practise gentle boundaries' exercise below to find out how.

Exercise: Practise gentle boundaries

Take a moment to read back through the section on in-laws (*see* pp. 102–5). Now pause.

What's one thing your in-laws have asked or said that made you feel uncomfortable, overwhelmed or small? Now, write down a gentle phrase – just one line you could say next time to protect your boundary with calm and clarity. It doesn't have to be perfect. It just has to be *yours*.

Here are some examples if you feel stuck:

- 'I appreciate your concern, but I've got this handled.'
- 'That doesn't work for me right now, but thank you for understanding.'
- 'I need a bit of space for this decision.'

Case studies – family relationships and marriage

As we've discussed, redefining marriage doesn't mean rejecting your family or your culture. It means finding a way to honour your roots while staying true to yourself. You can embrace the beauty of South Asian traditions, like celebrating occasions together or valuing family bonds, while leaving behind the parts that don't serve you. To explore this further, let's take a look at how the idea of marriage played out for three of my clients in the case studies below.

> ## Case study
>
> ### Amina resents her parents' inaction
>
> Amina is 28 and the eldest daughter in her British Pakistani household. She's a teacher, and she's spent years carrying the weight of financial responsibilities and caregiving duties for her younger siblings. Her father doesn't earn enough, which leaves Amina feeling like the second mother in the house, managing tasks that no one else can. Alongside this, she faces immense pressure to get married, with constant questions from extended family about why she hasn't found anyone yet. While Amina wants to get married, these questions led to a deep sense of resentment that she struggled to process.
>
> She resents her parents for not fulfilling what she felt were their responsibilities – *why didn't they help her, particularly when she was younger, and why didn't they find her a spouse?* Her strict upbringing meant she wasn't allowed to engage with boys, and that caused further confusion and anger as she grew older. Amina believes her parents expect her to continue running the home, but, out of shame, they will never openly say this. She told me, 'I just know deep down they want me to stay here. They need me, but they don't say it. I'm stuck.'
>
> Amina is deeply conflicted. She doesn't understand why, after being told to stay away from men because her parents would find her a spouse, they didn't do that. She feels it's now too late for her, and her life has become confined to either serving her family or going to work. 'I want to get married,' she says. 'I want a life for myself, but it feels impossible now. I don't know where to even start looking.'
>
> The tension between what she desires and the family dynamics has left Amina in an emotional limbo. Amina feels her parents don't see her as a person with her own hopes and desires. Instead, she feels like a burden to be managed. 'I can't talk to them about marriage. I don't want to look desperate. But I feel trapped, I feel invisible,' she concludes. The confusion and resentment she feels towards her parents, who both shaped her world and held her back, leaves her struggling to find a path forward, torn between the life she wants and the role she's been forced to play.

Case study

Khadija's family ignore what she wants

Khadija is 30, British Bangladeshi and a nurse. She's been struggling with depression and low self-esteem for the past five years. Her emotional exhaustion stems from the constant rejection of her own preferences by her parents when it comes to choosing a potential partner. Despite her desire to have control over this significant decision, Khadija feels trapped in a system where her parents make all the choices, despite their history of poor decisions. She shared, 'What's the point of getting to know someone if my parents are just going to say no? It's like I'm just wasting my time.'

This has led Khadija to a place where she no longer wants to pursue marriage. Instead, she's focusing on herself, but that comes with a deep sense of regret. She often says, 'I feel like I missed out on my youth. My friends were out there living their lives, making memories, and I was just focused on this marriage thing.' She now feels disconnected from her friends, unable to relate to their experiences of freedom and independence.

The pressure from her family to accept their choices has silenced her: 'They always say, "Your parents choose the best for you," but what about what I want? What about my happiness?' This constant dismissal of her own needs has left her feeling isolated from both her family and her friends, building up a deep sense of resentment towards her parents. She feels that they have, in her words, 'ruined my life.'

Khadija's case is a painful example of the way in which control and the neglect of individual desires can trap someone in emotional turmoil. She's struggling to find her own path, disconnected from the life she wanted and haunted by the feeling that her own voice was never heard.

Case study

Yusra sees marriage as her only escape

Yusra, a 22-year-old British-Indian student, came to therapy struggling with low moods and anxiety, and it quickly became clear that her home environment was playing a significant role in her distress. She described her childhood as being shaped by constant arguments and fights between her parents – a chaotic and traumatic backdrop that left her feeling emotionally drained.

As she explained, 'My parents, they fight all the time. Screaming, slamming doors – it's like I've been living in a battle my whole life.' Yusra shared that she spends most of her time isolated in her room, using her studies as an escape. 'When I'm at university, buried in books, at least I can pretend for a little while that I'm not trapped. But then I come home and it all starts again.' The rare moments she spends outside the house bring her some relief, but the suffocating atmosphere of her home is always there in the background.

One of the most heartbreaking aspects of Yusra's story is her silence. She feels unable to open up to her friends about her struggles: *'I don't want to burden them. My friends don't know what it's like. I don't want to be the one who always has problems.'* She carries immense guilt whenever she speaks about her parents, even to herself, as though acknowledging the pain they've caused is an act of betrayal: 'I feel so guilty even saying this, but I hate how they make me feel. Like I don't exist, like I'm just there to watch them tear each other apart.' This guilt keeps her trapped in a cycle of loneliness, unable to process her emotions or seek support.

What's particularly concerning is Yusra's belief that marriage is her only way out. In her words, 'I won't have to feel as suffocated. I can start afresh with a new family.' For Yusra, the idea of living independently is not an option. It goes against the cultural norms she's been raised with, where leaving the family home without marriage is seen as unacceptable. She sees marriage not as a partnership or a connection but as a lifeline, allowing her to escape from her current reality. However, this perception raises critical questions about what marriage would actually mean for her if entered into from a place of such emotional pain and unresolved trauma.

Yusra's story highlights the complex intersection of cultural expectations, family dynamics and personal mental health. It's a painful reminder of how deeply internalised guilt, shame and a lack of emotional safety can shape a person's decisions and beliefs about their future.

Looking at the three real-life examples above, we can see that they reflect very different experiences, but can you spot any common themes? What stands out for you? Brown children often feel immense guilt at the thought of upsetting their parents, so they end up suppressing all their emotions deep in their body. I regularly work with my clients on how to gently make space for this guilt alongside other emotions, and I want to remind you of the following:

- It's okay to acknowledge how your experiences have impacted you *and* to still love your parents.
- Acknowledging the impact of your parents' actions does *not* mean you hate your parents and caregivers.
- You can love your parents *and* understand they may get it wrong sometimes.
- Perhaps your life hasn't turned out the way you thought, but you hold the power to choose what you want your life to look like now.

Use the exercise below to help you sort through some of the issues raised in this chapter so far.

Exercise: Pausing for reflection

Grab your journal and write down your answers to the following questions (you don't have to answer them all if they don't feel relevant or if they aren't yet comfortable):

- If you could define freedom, what would that mean for you?
- Reflect on any past relationships – family, friends or romantic – where you felt invisible or unheard. What would it take for you to feel seen and understood in those relationships now?
- What expectations did your family place on you growing up, and how do they continue to influence your life today?
- Think about moments in your life when you felt like you couldn't speak up or express your desires. How can you start advocating for your own voice moving forward? What might that look like in your relationships with your family or others?
- How can you allow yourself to experience living and enjoying the present moment?
- Thinking beyond marriage as an escape, what else can it mean? How do you define companionship?

Bodily autonomy

Many women who come to see me have been married for years but still think intimacy is about one, not two, people – that it's about satisfying your partner instead of being an act of love and connection between both of you. If you were lucky, you might have had an elder sister who finally broached the subject and passed on some information, but even she probably acquired that information after she was married.

There's a lot of shame – a word I'll use often in this section – around topics like intimacy and menstruation (see box on p. 136), to the point where we don't even think to educate girls about these subjects, but it's time to break the silence. For far too long, we've been made to feel ashamed of our bodies, taught to see our natural rhythms as inconvenient and our desires as shameful, but there's nothing shameful about understanding your body or advocating for your needs.

Intimacy isn't a duty; it's a shared experience that should bring you comfort, safety and connection. Knowing your body isn't immodest – it's empowering. When you understand how your menstrual cycle affects your mood, energy and well-being, you can care for yourself with more compassion. You can also communicate your needs to your partner, creating a more empathetic and considerate relationship.

Your pleasure and comfort matter just as much as your partner's. True intimacy cannot thrive in silence or shame. It needs open communication, emotional safety and mutual care. You should never feel pressured into intimacy out of fear, guilt or obligation. You have the right to say 'no', to express what feels good and to be met with respect. The belief that men's needs come first while you quietly endure is a lie that's been passed down through generations. You don't have to inherit it. You deserve to feel safe in your body, informed about your needs and free to experience intimacy as something that belongs to you – not something you owe. A question I often ask my clients is: 'Do you feel safe enough to say "no" before you say "yes"?' Take the first steps with the 'Exploring your desires without shame' exercise below.

Exercise: Exploring your desires without shame

- **Create a safe space for self-exploration:** Ask yourself:
  - *What makes me feel safe and cared for?*

- *When do I feel most connected to my body?* (For example, after a shower, while dancing, during movement)
- *What kind of affection or touch feels comforting?* (For example, a hand on your back, gentle hugs)

- **Challenge internalised shame:** If you catch yourself feeling guilty for having emotional or physical desires, pause and reframe your thoughts. Gently remind yourself, *My needs are valid. My desires are not shameful.* It takes time to unlearn this conditioning, so be patient with yourself.

As you explore your body, your needs and your desires, remember that there's no shame in wanting to feel good, emotionally, physically and intimately. You're not here to simply endure or serve. You're here to experience love, safety and connection in a way that honours your whole being. You deserve nothing less.

Your menstrual cycle

Your period isn't just a monthly inconvenience. Learning to track and understand your menstrual cycle can help you tune into your body's natural patterns, recognise your needs and practice self-compassion:

- **Track your cycle:** Use a journal or a simple period tracking app (Clue or Moody Month) to note down the start and end of your period. Pay attention to physical symptoms (cramps, fatigue or tenderness) and emotional shifts (mood swings, irritability or low energy).
- **Notice your energy and desire patterns:** You may find that you feel more energetic and social during your follicular phase (after your period) and more introspective or sensitive during your luteal phase (before your period). During ovulation, you may feel more physically drawn to intimacy. Recognising these patterns helps you be kinder to yourself and communicate your needs more clearly.
- **Give yourself permission to rest:** Instead of pushing through fatigue during your period, allow yourself more rest. Let your partner know what kind of support you need. This is self-care, not weakness.

Handling divorce

Dear Brown girls, relationships can break down – some after a few months, others after years. It doesn't make you a failure. It's not up to you alone to make a marriage work, and sometimes things are beyond your control. The person who wasn't a good fit for you might just be a good fit for someone else, and the same applies to you.

So, allow yourself to choose you. Allow yourself to be seen. Dismantling these negative views will help others view you for who you are. Divorced? So what? You've been given a chance to live for yourself again.

It's unfortunate that so much pressure is placed on women to stay in a marriage just to avoid being labelled a divorcée. It's even more catastrophic to see how many lives are lost because women are too afraid to speak up and so stay in abusive relationships.

As a society, we don't make it easy for Brown girls. We're highly judgemental about anything out of the 'norm'. If you stay, you're foolish for staying; if you leave, you haven't tried hard enough. Sometimes, it feels like we can never win.

When you've grown up being told marriage is forever, even if it's unbearable, the idea of divorce can feel impossible. You might hear voices in your head saying things like, *What will people say? How will I manage on my own?* and *I'll bring shame to my family.* You need to decide whether staying in a marriage where you're not loved, respected or valued will be more damaging than leaving. Divorce isn't about giving up but about standing up. It's about saying, 'I deserve better than this.' Leaving is never a failure; it's an act of courage.

When a marriage is toxic, whether it's filled with emotional neglect, abuse or simply a lack of love, staying can be at the cost of your mental health, your peace and your sense of self. Divorce is a way of saying, 'I refuse to sacrifice myself for the sake of appearances.'

Choosing yourself isn't selfish; it's survival. And while the journey might feel lonely at first, it's a path that leads to healing, growth and, eventually, joy. You're not responsible for the expectations of others. You're responsible for your own happiness – and sometimes, that means walking away.

DEALING WITH THE FALLOUT

The aftermath of divorce can feel like a whirlwind. You might feel grief for the relationship you hoped would last forever. You might feel anger towards your ex-partner or even towards yourself for staying as long as you did. You might feel lost, unsure of who you are outside your marriage. And you might even fear the financial implications that come with a divorce.

Feeling lost is a huge one. You grew up being told you could rely on your partner to look after you, so you may believe that, in order to live, you need someone else. That is far from the truth. You have a community – and if you don't, then it's time to build one.

Allow yourself to grieve for what you'd planned for your future, and allow yourself to feel the pain of betrayal. It's all valid, so allow yourself to sit with your emotions. While it's true that the road might feel lonely or uncertain, there's always light, because you chose you for once. You have the strength to rebuild, to reclaim and to redefine what happiness looks like for you.

Remember, healing doesn't mean forgetting. It means learning to carry the pain in a way that doesn't weigh you down. Yes, there will be people who judge you. Yes, there will be whispers and raised eyebrows, but those voices don't matter. What matters is *your* voice. You faced one of the hardest decisions imaginable and chose to honour yourself.

What if honour wasn't about being the perfect daughter, wife or mother but about being the most authentic version of yourself? Honour can mean standing up for yourself when others try to silence you. Honour can mean leaving a toxic relationship, even if it goes against what's expected. Honour can mean living a life that feels true to you, even if it looks different from the one your family imagined. Honour can mean voicing your experiences and saying, 'No more'.

The cycle of shame and honour isn't something that started with your parents – it's been passed down for generations. And while it's easy to feel resentment towards family members who perpetuate these ideas, it's also important to understand where they're coming from.

For many of our parents and grandparents, shame and honour were survival tools. In a world where community approval could mean the difference between acceptance and isolation, they did what they thought was necessary to protect themselves. But times have changed, and so must the rules. Too many have suffered in silence; we've seen strained relationships, and we've seen people's mental and physical health deteriorating.

One of the hardest parts of breaking the shame and honour cycle is learning to let go of what others think of you. The truth is, no matter what you do, there will always be someone who disapproves. If you live for their approval, you'll never truly live for yourself.

Divorce isn't an ending; it's a new beginning. It's a decision to choose yourself when the world tells you to stay in pain. It's not easy, and it's certainly not celebrated in our culture, but for many women it's the first step towards freedom. It's maybe a few chapters in your story, not the whole book, so don't let it define the whole you. The 'Reframing divorce' exercise below is designed to help you rethink what divorce means to you.

Exercise: Reframing divorce

This exercise invites you to meet yourself, not through the lens of what you've lost but through who you are becoming.

Part 1: Unlearning the Inherited Narrative
Write down two to three messages you were taught (explicitly or silently) about divorce, growing up. These could sound like the following:

- 'A divorced woman brings shame to her family.'
- 'No one will want you after this.'
- 'Good women stay, no matter what.'

Pause and look at them. Whose voice do you hear behind those messages? A mother? A father? Society? Now, beside each one, write a counter-truth – something you're learning to believe now. For example:

- 'I am not a source of shame. I'm someone who survived.'
- 'I am still lovable, worthy and whole.'

Part 2: Naming Your Becoming
Now complete this sentence: 'Divorce didn't take me away from myself, it brought me closer to the version of me who. . .'

Let yourself finish this sentence in your own words. Maybe one of the following resonates:

- '. . . trusts her intuition.'
- '. . . chooses peace over performance.'
- '. . . knows her worth is not up for debate.'

Dear Brown girls, you are not here to fix what they think of you. You are here to become more of yourself.

You call the shots

I want to finish this chapter by reminding you that Brown women are thriving. Many have forged brilliant careers, pursued their dreams and created lives full of meaning and purpose. They've balanced the stringent demands of marriage, motherhood and family expectations, all while excelling in their professional lives. Yes, it's true that there's always this unspoken belief that no matter how much someone achieves or how far they go, it isn't as important or worthwhile as getting married – but despite the weight of this narrative, they've pushed through.

Whether you choose marriage, a career or a life path entirely your own, your choices are yours, and you are allowed to decide what's central for you. None of it is easy, yet here you are – resilient, powerful and living proof that South Asian women are more than the roles assigned to them. Brown girls, *you are extraordinary*.

4. Who do you blame? Slowly breaking the cycle

I've been a therapist for over 13 years, and I've noticed a stage many people reach on their healing journey: *blame*. After moving through waves of anger, sadness and pain, you might find yourself stuck in this stage, looking for someone you can hold responsible for the difficulties in your life and the agony you feel. You may blame your parents for not protecting you, for being emotionally unavailable or for imposing cultural expectations that left you feeling unseen. You may blame the community for its judgement, for forcing you into roles that made you uncomfortable or for stripping away your self-esteem. You might even blame yourself, questioning why you tolerated certain things for so long.

Blame feels heavy and complicated. It can make the emotional toll of growing up in a Brown household, shaped by silent rules and patterns of behaviour handed down from parents to children, feel too much to carry. In this chapter, I want to introduce you to the concept of generational trauma. When you reach this stage of the healing process, you're not just blaming individuals; you're grappling with inherited pain, passed down through familial and cultural customs and practices. This chapter will guide you through the blame stage. It will help you understand that the weight you're carrying may not have started with you – and, more importantly, show you how to begin releasing the blame.

The Traditional Narrative

Before you can move forward, you need to understand something important – something you may have felt your whole life but didn't have the words for. It's called generational trauma, and it's when pain, fear and modes of survival are passed down from one generation to the next: through the way you were raised, through the things that could never be spoken about, through the silences. Generational trauma rarely comes up in conversation. It's like carrying invisible luggage that was packed long before you were even born.

If you grew up in a Brown family, the chances are you've felt the weight of generational trauma. It shows up in the way you were taught to love, to cope, to dream, to survive. This isn't because your parents or grandparents were bad people but because they lived through so much – colonialism, Partition, migration, poverty, patriarchy – and they had to survive. When survival is the focus, emotional needs often come last. Pain, fear and shame are transmitted to the next generation without anyone realising it, like a package quietly placed into your hands without warning.

Carrying this kind of trauma leaves real scars, even if you can't always see them:

- It can make you feel anxious even when you're safe.
- It can make you feel guilty for saying 'no'.
- It can make conflict feel terrifying, even when you're just standing up for yourself.
- It can make love and connection feel confusing, heavy or out of reach.

If you've ever found yourself freezing when an elder raises their voice, swallowing a response to avoid upsetting others or feeling torn between your own needs and your family's expectations, you're not imagining it. This is the emotional and psychological impact of wounds that were inflicted long before you were born. Generational trauma ties together everything we discuss in this book: it is living in our bodies and nervous systems. Yet, we can begin unlearning old patterns and start regulating differently.

Understanding generational trauma

Generational trauma is the thread that binds you to the unexpressed pain of those who came before you. It isn't limited to your lifetime; it's the unresolved wounds, fears and struggles carried by your parents, grandparents and even earlier generations, often without ever being named or addressed. Certain events left emotional scars that didn't end with the people who experienced them but were absorbed into family dynamics, behaviours and beliefs, shaping how we live and relate to one another today.

Think of how scarcity may manifest in your family. If your grandparents suffered through war, displacement or poverty, they might have developed a scarcity mindset – an ingrained fear of not having enough. That fear gets passed down, not necessarily through words but through actions: strictness around money, constant reminders to save for the future or pressure to choose 'safe' careers instead of pursuing passions. The message might sound like, 'You'll never survive as a...' or 'You can't afford to take risks.' On the surface, this feels like a lack of support, but beneath it is a generational fear of losing stability.

Generational trauma also bleeds into how emotions are expressed or suppressed. If your parents were raised in environments where survival came before emotional connection, they may have learned to suppress their own feelings and then unintentionally, or possibly intentionally, taught you to do the same. A parent who grew up in survival mode might tell you, *'Stop crying and be strong'* – not because they don't care, but because they were never allowed to express vulnerability themselves. This leaves you questioning your own emotions: *I feel so much, but why am I not allowed to show it?* or *Why can't I name what's going on inside me?*

It also appears in the way in which love is given or withheld. A parent who grew up in a home where affection wasn't openly expressed might struggle to praise or validate you, even if they care for you deeply. Instead of being more direct, they might tell you things like, 'You should just know I'm proud of you.' This can leave you feeling unseen, unappreciated or even unloved, even though the root of this withholding isn't personal; it's historical. South Asian families often wrap this pain in layers of silence, shame or strict cultural expectations, making it even harder to address. The result is a cycle of unspoken hurt that feels impossible to break.

When you recognise these patterns, it's easy to feel frustration or anger towards your family. You might think, *Why couldn't they just do better?* But the reality is, generational trauma often operates in ways that are invisible to the people living it. Most of our elders didn't have access to therapy, language or tools to process their pain. They carried what they could, passing down survival strategies alongside their wounds. Their struggles weren't meant to harm you; they were simply the only way they knew how to cope.

Understanding generational trauma doesn't mean excusing harmful behaviour, but it does mean seeing the bigger picture. It means acknowledging that your pain exists within a larger story of resilience, survival and unspoken sorrow. You're now part of a generation that has the tools to name these patterns, the courage to untangle them and the opportunity to break cycles of trauma. This is the beginning of healing – not just for yourself but for the generations that come after you. You are creating space for something new: love, freedom and connection unburdened by the past.

Because I said so

The roles of parents, elders and authority figures in Brown households are often seen as sacred and unquestionable. From a young age, children are taught that respect for elders is fundamental, not optional, but this respect isn't just about politeness; it's about obeying without question, even when decisions or behaviours feel unfair or hurtful. The phrase 'They're your elders; they know best' becomes a default response, shutting down any room for examination or dialogue.

This cultural hierarchy can make it difficult to express your needs or set boundaries. For instance, if a parent insists you follow a certain life path, you might feel silenced, either because speaking up is seen as disrespectful or simply because they have been on this earth longer, so you can't know better than them. Likewise, if a family elder makes hurtful comments about your life choices, appearance or relationships, you may feel obligated to endure them, because confrontation is viewed as dishonouring their status.

The traditional narrative often places elders at the top of a pyramid where their authority is absolute. Their experiences are seen as more valuable than your feelings or perspectives, and challenging them is interpreted as a personal attack rather than part of a discussion. Even when elders make mistakes or perpetuate harmful behaviours, the expectation is that you tolerate them silently, because they've 'earned' their authority through age or sacrifice.

For example, if you express frustration about a controlling parent or an intrusive in-law, you might be told, 'They did everything for you – the least you can do is listen to them.' While it's true that many elders have made sacrifices, this narrative often dismisses your lived experiences. It can leave you feeling trapped: wanting to honour their efforts but also feeling unheard and invalid. You might sit and think, *Well, what about me then?*

This dynamic isn't limited to elders such as parents or uncles but often extends to older siblings as well. The family hierarchy is so rigid that the position of being an older sibling often comes with an unearned sense of authority. Their age alone can invalidate your perspective, creating a power dynamic that feels unjust. It's as though the title of 'older sibling' automatically gives them the right to offer unsolicited advice, override your opinions and make decisions, regardless of whether their words or actions are reasonable. This unspoken rule can be frustrating, especially when older siblings are treated as if they can do no wrong or their mistakes are quietly overlooked.

What makes this dynamic even more challenging is the emotional weight it carries. Questioning an older sibling's choices or behaviour can sometimes be perceived as disrespectful, regardless of how you express yourself. This reinforces a cycle where their authority remains unchallenged and your voice is diminished. Over time, this can create resentment, a sense of invisibility or even self-doubt, as you begin to internalise the idea that your opinions or experiences carry less value simply because of your position in the family.

Of course, you yourself may be an older sibling, and you may hold your own resentments. The eldest child role may not sit well with you: you may feel that your parents were stricter with you than with your siblings or that you were given responsibilities you didn't want and therefore had to grow up more quickly. As the eldest, you probably don't see yourself as overbearing or dismissive, and you may genuinely believe you have guided and protected your younger brothers and sisters. Wherever you come in the family hierarchy, it's important to recognise that your role isn't always about intentional power or control but is often a by-product of cultural norms that emphasise age and authority. Understanding this can help us all approach family dynamics with empathy while also advocating for our own voice and boundaries.

While these hierarchies may have been rooted in tradition and originally emerged to maintain order and respect, often they fail to adapt to changing times and circumstances. As a result, they can leave many Brown women feeling powerless, unable to articulate their struggles or make independent choices, and often create distant, strained family relationships where interactions are polite but shallow.

Shame as a deflection tool

In many family dynamics, shame acts as a powerful deflection tool. This is particularly the case in Brown families, where avoiding criticism and maintaining honour are deeply rooted values. Instead of an issue being addressed with empathy or curiosity, shame redirects the focus away from accountability and places blame on the individual who dares to question, struggle or express themselves. This deflection not only silences the person at the centre of the discussion but also reinforces the cycle of blame, ensuring that the root issue remains unaddressed.

For instance, when a child voices their struggles or challenges, they might be met with responses like, 'How could you say that? Do you know how hard we've worked for you?' or 'What will people think if they hear you talking like this?' These statements immediately shift the focus away from the child's feelings and on to the family's perceived reputation or sacrifice. The underlying message is clear: your emotions or needs are secondary to preserving the image of the family. This tactic effectively shuts down dialogue and deflects any responsibility away from the person or system causing harm.

Shame as a deflection tool also creates a pattern where blame is passed rather than resolved. For example:

- A parent who is unable to process their own insecurities or mistakes may deflect by shaming a child for their choices, saying things like, 'You're so ungrateful' or 'You don't understand our struggles.'
- In sibling dynamics, one sibling might deflect responsibility for their actions by shaming the other, perhaps by saying, 'You're always so sensitive' or 'You're the problem in this family.'

- Even broader cultural expectations, like the pressure to conform to societal norms around marriage or career, use shame as a tool to deflect from systemic issues via comments such as, 'Don't embarrass the family' or 'Why aren't you married yet?'

This deflection not only reinforces the original issue but ensures it is repeated. Instead of addressing the core problem - be it miscommunication, unmet emotional needs or systemic pressures - shame shifts the focus to the individual, isolating them and making them feel as though they are the problem. This results in a lack of understanding and resolution. When shame is used as a weapon, it prevents meaningful conversations and emotional growth. The person on the receiving end of shame learns to internalise this shame, often questioning their own worth or silencing their needs to avoid further blame. Meanwhile, those using shame remain stuck in their own cycles of deflection, unable to see their role in perpetuating harm.

Handling conflict

It's clear that in many South Asian households, people can really struggle to handle conflicts effectively. This often leads to strained family ties, broken relationships with siblings and lost friendships. I've noticed that the inability to navigate disagreements or express themselves can leave individuals feeling trapped and suffocated.

If you feel that way, it's probably because you didn't learn healthy conflict resolution strategies while growing up. In fact, I'm sure many of you observed unproductive ways of managing conflicts, like giving people the silent treatment, having shouting matches and even instances of physical abuse. This commonly leads to the avoidance of confrontation, which allows blame and resentment to build up; as a result, unresolved issues may resurface later, even long after you've moved out, resulting in emotionally charged conversations where, again, you struggle to feel truly listened to.

It's no surprise that you might find conflict hard to deal with now if you grew up in a home where it meant shouting, slamming doors or long silences that stretched for days. And when that's your early environment, the desire to sidestep confrontation doesn't just disappear – it follows you into your relationships, your workplace and the way you treat yourself. You might find that:

- you avoid conflict at all costs, even when something's hurting you;
- you shut down emotionally when someone's upset with you;
- you struggle to express your needs or say how you feel, especially if it might cause tension;
- you feel intense anxiety before or after difficult conversations;
- you assume conflict always means something's going terribly wrong rather than being something that can be worked through;
- you swing between silence and snapping, unsure how else to cope;
- you feel guilty or ashamed for bringing issues up, as if you're causing trouble just by being honest.

A typical scenario might be as follows. You let your mum know you won't be able to make it to a family gathering that weekend because you're exhausted. She says, 'Everyone else's children make time for their families. We must have done something wrong raising you.' The guilt hits you in your chest. You start justifying yourself and overexplaining, or you just go quiet and think, *What's the point in even trying to speak up?*

Another scenario might be that you tell your husband you're thinking about starting therapy because you want to work on your anxiety, or maybe even unlearn some of the patterns you picked up while growing up. He looks at you and says, 'What will people think? You know how our families are. Just pray. It'll help more than any therapist.' You feel misunderstood. You're not dismissing faith – you just wanted support, to be heard not fixed – but now you're second-guessing yourself. You wonder if maybe you *are* being too sensitive. Maybe you *should* just cope quietly like the women before you. So, you stay quiet. Again.

It's quite possible that you find yourself reacting to situations with the same fear or defensiveness you had as a child, even now you're safe, independent and trying to do things differently. And it's not just about you. When you're around other people from South Asian communities – not just partners, but friends and even colleagues – they may also exhibit similar patterns of behaviour. You might notice the following:

- Conflict is dismissed or brushed aside: 'It's not a big deal; just forget it.'

- People take things very personally, even when you're being respectful.
- Disagreements are seen as disrespectful per se, but especially if they're directed at elders.
- Silence is used as a form of control, not resolution.
- Apologies are rare, because saying sorry was never modelled or expected (see below).

> ### Sorry is the hardest word
>
> In my work as a therapist, I've found that many people from Brown backgrounds struggle to accept apologies from their parents. The cultural norm of elders not apologising to those younger than them means that when a parent does offer an apology to a child, it can evoke complex emotions – particularly shame and guilt – in the child.
>
> This is partly because being apologised to by a parent is so unfamiliar that it makes the child feel guilty, sometimes because of the conditioning that 'elders do no wrong'. However, more fundamentally, instead of just wanting to hear the word 'sorry', what children are usually seeking from their parents is genuine acknowledgement: the space to express themselves and to be truly seen and understood. When a basic apology falls short of this, the child is left feeling resentful, which perpetuates (rather than breaks) the cycle of blame.

WHERE TO DRAW THE LINE

Boundaries are frequently mentioned on social media, but they're not always fully explained. In any relationship, boundaries are the limits you set – explicitly or implicitly – to protect your emotional well-being, your mental and physical space and perhaps your time as well. Boundaries work in the same way in family relationships, defining the way in which we interact with each other, the roles we play and how much autonomy we have. They're important because they help raise understanding and respect, support clear communication and make us all feel safe.

Boundaries are a normal part of all relationships, but in many South Asian homes they're misunderstood, and they can also look different in the Brown community. You might have been taught that setting boundaries is rude, unkind or even selfish, but that's not true. Boundaries aren't about pushing people away; they're about looking after yourself while still showing care for others.

The truth is, boundaries have always been there, even if no one called them that. Think about your mother, for example. Maybe she always cooked for guests or looked after everyone without ever saying she was tired or needed help. Maybe she stayed quiet, but you could tell, in her face, her body or her sighs, that she was worn out. Those were her boundaries being crossed. She might not have felt able to say 'no', and maybe she was determined to avoid conflict, but just because someone doesn't state their boundaries out loud doesn't mean they don't have them. Sometimes, it just means they don't feel safe enough to voice them, which is the situation my client Alina finds herself in (*see below*).

Case study

Financial responsibility creates resentment for Alina

Alina, a 26-year-old Pakistani woman, carries the weight of her family's expectations like a heavy shawl draped over her shoulders. She lives at home and works full time. As the eldest child, she feels immense pressure to be the glue that holds her family together, especially in a household filled with tension and constant arguments. Growing up, Alina was no stranger to the sound of her parents clashing, their voices raised over financial struggles that seemed to drown out any moments of joy.

In her therapy sessions, Alina revealed her deep desire to make her parents proud. She wants to put an end to their relentless fighting, to be the one who brings peace to their home. Yet beneath that longing lies a painful resentment. She struggles with conflicting emotions towards her father, who sends money overseas yet neglects to provide for the financial and emotional needs of her mother – but her mother, whom she loves deeply, seems to enable this behaviour, adding to Alina's frustration.

As an adult, Alina finds herself paying the family's rent, buying shopping and supporting her mother financially, yet her father remains largely absent in his contributions. This dynamic creates a heavy burden on her heart: she feels torn between her responsibilities and

→

> her own desires. Every time she opens her wallet, she battles the guilt of spending money on herself, questioning whether she deserves even a small treat when her parents' needs loom large in her mind.
>
> In many Brown households, fathers are seen as financially responsible for their wives and children. So, Alina feels that she's playing the role of the father, and she also feels unseen and unacknowledged by her parents – as if her sacrifices and efforts vanish into thin air. Their scrutiny of her finances only deepens her sense of inadequacy, reinforcing the belief that no matter how hard she tries, it will never be enough. The emotional toll is intense. Each moment of joy is overshadowed by guilt, each achievement feels tarnished by the weight of her family's expectations. But Alina's needs matter too. It's okay for her to seek her own life, and breaking the cycle of familial obligation may lead to the freedom she craves.

If Alina's story resonates with you, you're not alone. Many Brown women find themselves navigating complex family dynamics and encountering frequent conflicts. Acknowledging this reality is the first step towards understanding your own feelings and experiences. Reflect on the following questions:

- Have you ever felt the pressure to be the peacekeeper in your family, like you must hold everything together?
- Do you ever sacrifice your own needs to meet the demands of those around you, and, if so, how frequently does this happen?
- When was the last time you felt truly seen and appreciated for your efforts, and how did that make you feel?
- How often do you prioritise your own happiness amid your family's expectations?
- Are there moments when you've felt guilty for wanting to pursue your own dreams or even spend money on yourself?

It's okay to acknowledge that the dynamics at home can be challenging. Your feelings of frustration, resentment and even guilt are valid. They stem from a place of love and responsibility, but they can also lead to emotional exhaustion. However, by honouring the emotions that arise from these dynamics, you can begin to explore what changes might be necessary for your own well-being.

Where do you put the blame?

What would you say if I asked you who you hold responsible for what's happened to you, for what you went through, for the person who's struggling today? Perhaps your mind goes straight to your parents. They were supposed to be your safe space, your role models, your light. Maybe they made sure you were fed, dressed and educated, but no one asked how you were really feeling. And when someone disrespected you – an uncle, an auntie, even someone at home – you were expected to stay quiet, not to cause trouble, to keep the peace. They were meant to do better, to be better, and yet they didn't and weren't. I get it.

But maybe it's not just them. Maybe it's your extended family, the people who stood by and said nothing. Maybe it's the community, the culture or even the entire system that came up with the invisible life guide that made it impossible for you to feel seen or safe. Maybe, in moments of anger and pain, you blame everyone. Maybe you sit with this overwhelming feeling: *I blame everyone for everything.*

But listen to this: what you went through, whatever it was, should not have happened. You deserved better. You deserved a home where you felt protected, where the adults around you took responsibility for their actions, where they provided a safe environment for you to grow and thrive. You deserved adults who knew better, who understood the weight of their decisions, who didn't simply repeat cycles of toxicity and harm. Because isn't that the bare minimum?

After all, they chose to have you, didn't they? They decided to bring a child into the world, so why didn't they do better? Something I hear time and time again from survivors of abuse is this: 'They chose to have me – I didn't say to bring me to this world.' When I hear that, I hear deep pain and anger.

I know how confusing and enraging it can be. How could the very people who should have shielded you from pain perpetuate it themselves? How could they carry forward toxic, unhealthy behaviours when they hated some of those same things in their own lives? It doesn't make sense, does it? And that lack of sense, that lack of logic, makes it even harder to process.

Blame is often the first step towards understanding and unravelling the layers of what happened to you. It's part of naming the pain, and naming it is part of the process of freeing yourself from it. I promise I won't say to you, 'But they are your parents.' You don't have to understand it all right now, and you don't have to forgive anyone who hasn't earned it, but please know that your pain matters – and so do you.

Where were they when you needed them? This question doesn't fade. It lingers in the background of your life, shaping how you trust, how you love and how you protect yourself. But asking this question is about more than just pointing fingers; it's a way of expressing the deep hurt of being let down. It's naming what you were deprived of and, as painful as it is, it's also a step towards understanding that their absence wasn't your fault.

Blame is so much more than a cognitive process. It's a signal. It points to something deeper, something unresolved. When you notice yourself blaming, it's often because a boundary was crossed, a need wasn't met or an injustice occurred. It's your mind and body's way of saying, *This wasn't right – something here hurt me.*

Blame can feel heavy, and it's often accompanied by guilt or shame: *Should I even feel this way? Is it okay to blame my parents, my family or my culture?* But blame isn't inherently bad. It's a tool that helps you identify where things went wrong or where pain originated. For survivors of trauma, blame often gets a bad reputation. You're told to 'move on', to 'forgive and forget' or to 'focus on the positive', but how can you do that when you haven't even had the chance to unpack the weight of what happened?

Blame isn't something to suppress; it's something to explore. Who or what are you blaming? Why? What unmet needs or unresolved pain lie beneath that feeling? Blame, when acknowledged, can become a roadmap to understanding yourself better, but it isn't the final destination. It's a placeholder in your healing, not a permanent residence.

Case study

Leena learns to move past blame

When Leena first came to therapy, as a 26-year-old Indian women, she didn't come to heal; she came to vent. She sat across from me, listing every person who'd failed her: her mother who never listened, her father who only cared about his family back home, her sister who made everything about herself, the ex who'd betrayed her without explanation, her jealous friend. Her voice was steady, sharp and rehearsed, like she'd told this story a hundred times.

She wasn't wrong. Her pain was real. But every sentence ended with: 'It's because of them.' Over the weeks, I noticed how she clung to her anger. Whenever we gently explored her own patterns, she would say, 'I didn't get a choice. They made me this way.'

Then, one day, something shifted. We were talking about her father's emotional absence, and she said quietly, 'If I stop blaming him. . . I don't know who I am without the anger.' That moment cracked something open. It wasn't about letting anyone off the hook; it was about how much energy Leena had spent carrying everyone else's wrongdoing like bricks in her bag. She was exhausted from holding the weight.

We began to explore who she was beyond the story of being wronged. What did she need? What boundaries had never been allowed to exist? Slowly, she began to trade blame for curiosity and resentment for relief. She was learning that healing didn't mean forgetting; it meant finally putting the weight down.

Take a moment to ask yourself: *What weight am I still carrying that no longer belongs to me?*

Blame can feel like protection, but it often keeps you chained to pain. In your journal, reflect on one situation or relationship where you've felt stuck in resentment or blame. Without judging yourself, gently explore the following questions:

- *What am I holding onto in this story?*
- *What has blame given me?*
- *What might healing ask me to release?*

You don't need to have all the answers right now. This is simply a space to notice, with compassion, where you're still holding on and where you might one day be ready to let go.

BLAME AS A COPING MECHANISM

Blame is often the easiest response when we're faced with pain or injustice. It gives us something or someone to direct our emotions towards. In South Asian families, where emotions are often suppressed or dismissed, blame can be a hidden outlet for unspoken resentment, and it can feel like a way to regain control in a chaotic situation. When you're hurt by a parent's harsh words, when your in-laws' expectations feel suffocating or when cultural norms limit your individuality, it's natural to blame the people who seem closest to the issue.

For example, you might find yourself saying, 'If only my mother had been more supportive, I wouldn't struggle so much with self-doubt' or 'If my parents hadn't forced me into this career, I'd be living a happier life.' These thoughts feel valid because they connect your pain to its source. However, while it might feel empowering in the moment, blame is only part of the healing process.

Blame can also act as a shield or defence, because it's easier to point outwards than to face the complex web of generational trauma that contributes to our pain. However, holding on to blame can mean you remain preoccupied with what was done to you rather than how you can work through it. It's like clutching a stone in your hand: it gives you something solid to hold on to, but it also weighs you down.

It's human to look for someone to hold responsible for your pain, but the truth is, many of us get stuck in this place. Blame can become a comfortable story we tell ourselves: *It's all their fault – I am the way I am because of them.* While it might feel justified, staying in this mindset keeps you trapped, and the blame starts to shape your identity. It defines you as someone who was wronged, keeping you tied to the hurt rather than the healing.

Getting stuck in blame can also feel like a way of holding power over those who hurt you. If you've been silenced or invalidated for years, blaming others can feel like you've finally reclaimed your voice. However, continuing to blame keeps you emotionally tied to the very people or situations from which you want to free yourself. I know this feels hard to hear, but although it's common to see blame as the endpoint of healing, it's really just the beginning.

Dismantling The Traditional Narrative

The traditional narrative teaches us that our parents and elders acted out of love or survival, but their decisions also caused harm. You're left holding the weight of those decisions, wondering how to reconcile their struggles with the impact on your own life. This is where accountability with empathy comes in, because it's a way to hold space for both truths without invalidating your own pain.

However, it's easy to get stuck in the blame cycle without even realising it. When you've been hurt, especially by people you trusted like your parents, family or community, it's normal to focus on what they did wrong. That pain is real, and blaming them is a way to make sense of it. However, as I've said, staying in that space of blame, where your story is only about what others did to you, keeps you tied to their actions and stops you from seeing and stepping into the other parts of you.

Can we really dismantle generational trauma?

Now, before I talk about whether we can really dismantle generational trauma, I want to make it absolutely clear that I'm not another person telling you that your parents did the best they could, because I already know some of you will reply, 'No they didn't - they had choices and could have done more' - and I hear you. Or some of you may say, 'The more I understand my parents' feelings, the more guilty I will feel about living for myself.' Again, I hear you, but let me assure you that this isn't about making excuses for your parents' actions and it isn't about your guilt.

Accountability with empathy starts with recognising that generational trauma isn't just about what happened to you; it's also about what happened to them. Many South Asian parents grew up in environments where survival was the priority, whether due to financial instability, social restrictions or migration. They may never have had the chance to reflect on their emotions or learn how to break harmful patterns. This doesn't excuse the harm they caused, but it helps you see the context in which their behaviours developed.

For example, a parent who pressures you to prioritise security over passion might not be trying to control you - they may be projecting their own fears of instability or failure. A parent who withholds emotional warmth may not be intentionally trying to hurt you but repeating what they were taught about love and discipline. They may also believe that the world has been tough on them, so this is their way of teaching you to be tough in return. Accountability with empathy allows you to acknowledge this without dismissing how their actions affected you. It means holding them accountable for their behaviour while recognising that they, too, are products of their environment and upbringing. Your mother may never have given you a hug, yet she knew how to show her love by cooking you a meal. Your father may never have been present for you physically, yet his way of being present was by providing for you financially. These things can be true even if they weren't enough for you.

It's about freeing yourself from the emotional weight of resentment and blame. Empathy helps you understand that your parents' actions weren't always about you; they were often about their own unprocessed pain. Accountability ensures that you can still name the harm and set boundaries without excusing what happened. Together, they allow you to shift from a place of anger to one of understanding, which is key to breaking the cycle of trauma.

Generational trauma doesn't end with understanding alone. We can't just dismantle something that's generational, but we can shift things slowly through awareness. It ends when you decide to take a different path. You are the bridge between what has been and what can be. Yes, that's pressure, hence you're not expected to do it all alone, but we have to begin somewhere – and the fact that you've already decided you don't want to be part of something that hasn't served you is already a start. By holding your parents accountable with empathy, you're choosing to rewrite the narrative, not just for yourself but for future generations. 'The Family tree of patterns' exercise below will help you start to rewrite the narrative.

Exercise: The family tree of patterns

This visual tool will help you see generational trauma as a flow of experiences rather than just individual acts. It empowers you to recognise patterns, hold others accountable and focus on the changes you want to make, all while cultivating empathy for yourself and those who came before you:

1. **Draw your tree**
   - On a piece of paper, draw a tree with roots, a trunk and branches. The roots represent past generations, the trunk is your parents' generation and the branches are you and your siblings, or future generations.

2. **Identify the patterns**
   - In the roots, write down generational struggles – for example, financial hardship, emotional repression, migration.

- In the trunk, note the patterns you've observed in your parents' behaviours – for example, perfectionism, fear of failure, emotional distance.

3. **Add your experiences**
   - On the branches, write how these patterns have impacted you – for example, self-doubt, difficulty expressing emotions, need for external validation.

4. **Visualise the cycle**
   - Draw a dotted line connecting the roots, trunk and branches to represent how these patterns flow through the generations.

5. **Rewrite the narrative**
   - On the branches, write what you want to change – for example, 'I will prioritise emotional openness', 'I will choose a career I love', 'I will show love to my children.'
   - Highlight these changes in a different colour to symbolise breaking the cycle.

6. **Reflect on empathy and accountability**
   - Spend a few minutes looking at your tree. Ask yourself *What context shaped these patterns? What am I responsible for breaking? How can I honour my growth while holding others accountable?*

Authentic or rebellious?

One thing that's caught my attention is the common misconception that living authentically involves rebellion. It's intriguing to note that many people mistakenly conflate authenticity with rebelliousness. However, it's necessary to distinguish between the two concepts. Growing up in an environment where self-exploration was restricted and external influences heavily shaped your beliefs and decisions can make it challenging to achieve deep self-awareness, but living authentically is about genuinely connecting with and understanding yourself at a deep level. Authenticity is about changing and growing through experiences, but through these experiences you feel that you're doing right by and being honest with yourself.

While choosing to live authentically may lead to a form of rebellion against cultural or societal norms, it's important to understand that this rebellion doesn't embody authentic living. Instead, it often stems from a place of deep-seated resentment, anger and a desire to break free from those traditional expectations, but this rejection of aspects of your identity tends to be rooted in frustration and a rebellious stance against the status quo. It doesn't happen overnight, but I invite you to learn to love and accept all parts of you, rather than trying to 'fix' the issues within your family or 'change' your parents.

As a therapist, one of the things I want to highlight is that many parents are unable to acknowledge or validate what you've gone through because of their own emotional blocks. Their emotional block could be shame, embarrassment or a belief that they weren't a good enough mother or father. It may be that the only thing they can do is to become the victim in all of this, which again makes you feel as if there's no focus on you or prompts your guilt. These emotional blocks may be generational, and your parents may appear not to remember their own trauma because they feel defensive, are in denial or have chosen to forget it.

The following is an offering for you to ponder: how can you provide yourself with the nurturing and care you needed as a child? How can you address and heal from the pain you experienced in your childhood? It's common to reach a point in your personal growth journey where you feel compelled to heal your parents, but it's important to remember to focus on yourself. Focus inwards. I encourage you to stay present with your own emotions, validate your experiences and show yourself compassion. It's necessary to do so. Many people tend to avoid confronting their emotional pain and want to run away from themselves, but you need to make space for those feelings – forgive yourself for any past actions and reactions, and acknowledge the pain you've endured – and allow yourself to experience and process them. Use the 'Reflection and connection' exercise below to examine your intentions and connect with your true self.

Exercise: Reflection and connection

This exercise is designed to help you pause and reflect before taking an action or making a decision that feels difficult or emotionally charged:

1. **Ground yourself:** Before diving into your feelings, create a calm space to reflect. This might mean taking a few deep breaths, sitting

quietly or journalling your thoughts. You're creating a moment of pause to remove reactive energy. Close your eyes for a moment and visualise a tree with deep, stable roots. Imagine yourself grounding into those roots, connected to your values, emotions and history. This step is about calming any impulsive or defensive energy and preparing yourself to listen inwardly.

2. **Ask reflective questions**: Write down your answers to these questions, or think through them, to explore where your actions are coming from:
    - **What's driving this choice or feeling?** Ask yourself, *Am I acting from a place of hurt, anger or frustration with others?* or *Am I acting from a place of self-love, self-respect and personal alignment?* This helps you recognise whether you're reacting to external control (rebellion) or responding to internal truth (authenticity).
    - **Who benefits from this action?** *Am I doing this to prove something to someone else, even if it hurts me in the long run?* or *Am I doing this because it feels good, right and aligned with who I am, regardless of external approval?*
    - **Does this action align with my long-term values or goals?** Rebellion is often short term – an emotional response to someone or something. Authenticity honours your bigger picture, even when it's hard or uncomfortable.
    - **What emotions come up when I think about this?** Rebellion might feel like anger, defiance or spite. Authenticity, even if it's challenging, often feels like relief, peace or empowerment.

3. **Visualise the outcome:** Create two visual scenarios. First, imagine yourself making this decision purely to oppose someone or something. How do you feel afterwards? Do you feel lighter, or is the resistance still weighing on you? Now, imagine making this decision because it's aligned with your true desires and values. How do you feel in this scenario? Can you see yourself growing from this choice?

4. **Take one small authentic action:** Even if you're unsure whether your choice is rebellious or authentic, experiment with one small

step towards what feels true to you. Authenticity often feels freeing, even if it's scary, because it reflects your inner values rather than a reaction to others' expectations.

By practising this process, you'll start to notice patterns in your decisions. The more you pause, root and reflect, the clearer it will become whether you're acting out of rebellion or authenticity. This is a muscle you build over time, so give yourself patience and grace as you develop this self-awareness.

Balancing individuality and togetherness

For many of us, individuality wasn't something we were encouraged to explore. Maybe you were praised for how well you followed the rules or how much you sacrificed for others, but adhering to the good girl narrative is exhausting. It asks you to shrink yourself, to dim your light and to silence your voice. And for what? To make everyone else happy? Did it feel enough? Does it ever feel enough? No, really – does it?

You don't have to live up to this impossible standard. Being a good daughter, sister or partner doesn't mean losing yourself in the process. You can still be loving, caring and connected while also being bold, loud and unapologetically *you*. And this is where I invite you to understand the concept that two things can exist at the same time: togetherness doesn't have to mean losing your individuality.

Truly living is about showing up as your authentic self, not a version of you that fits neatly into someone else's expectations. When you hide parts of yourself to keep the peace, are you really connecting with others? Or are you just playing a role? Real togetherness is built on honesty, respect and mutual support. It's about creating space for everyone to be who they are, including you.

Due to the lessons you've absorbed, I know that showing up as your true self in an environment that favours the collective might seem selfish. It might also feel difficult, as you're probably still trying to figure out who you are – and that's okay, because the process of getting to know who you are really is a process. On the next page you'll find a couple of short exercises that you can do regularly to help that process along.

Exercise: Recognise your full self 🧩

Start by acknowledging that you can love your family, your culture and your community without sacrificing who you are. Remind yourself daily that your needs, desires and dreams are important, too, and it's not selfish to take up space in your own life.

Take action: Each day, ask yourself, *What would make me feel more like myself today?* Whether it's a hobby, a conversation or a moment of quiet, take time to nurture the parts of you that may have been overlooked.

Exercise: Embrace both/and 🧩

Finding the balance between individuality and family isn't about rejecting your culture or turning your back on your loved ones. It's about creating a life where you can respect both. You can be deeply connected to your family and community while still honouring your unique identity. Togetherness doesn't require you to shrink or silence parts of yourself.

Take action: Identify one area where you feel torn between family expectations and your own needs. Challenge yourself to find a way to honour both sides. For example, if you feel pressure to take on more responsibilities at home, set aside time for yourself to recharge first. Then you can return to your responsibilities from a place of strength, not depletion.

This balance between individuality and togetherness won't look the same for everyone, but try to communicate with honesty. Share your dreams and goals with your family, even if they don't fully understand or agree with them.

It's also sensible to choose your battles. Not every disagreement has to turn into a fight, and sometimes the best way to protect your individuality is to say nothing – particularly when you think the consequences would do more harm to your growth than good. The difference now is that you are *choosing* to stay silent rather than feeling *obligated* to be silent.

The end goal is to build a life that reflects you. Whether it's your career, your relationships or your hobbies, begin to make choices that align with your values, not just the ones handed down to you. Explore how to get started with 'The balance tool' exercise on the next page.

Exercise: The balance tool 🧩

This tool helps you assess where you might be over-investing in roles and reminds you to create space for your authentic self. Balancing both is a constant practice, but these small steps can lead to a healthier balance:

1. **List your current roles:** Write down the roles you play in your life (e.g. daughter, partner, friend, employee, caregiver).
2. **Identify your personal needs:** Write down what makes you feel most like *you* – your hobbies, alone time, passions or anything that helps you feel fulfilled outside your roles.
3. **Check for balance:** For each role you listed, ask yourself: *Am I giving enough space to my personal needs?* On a scale from 1 to 10, rate how well you feel you're balancing togetherness and individuality (with 1 being 'completely lost in roles' and 10 being 'perfectly balanced').
4. **Take action:** Choose one small action for each role you play and one way to nurture your individuality. For example, if your role as a daughter takes up a lot of energy, maybe schedule an hour to yourself each week to recharge. If you're nurturing a relationship, plan something for *just you*, like a hobby or a personal goal.
5. **Daily check-in:** Each day, ask yourself: *Am I making space for both connection with others and connection with myself today?*

As you start to reclaim your individuality, you might feel a mix of excitement and fear. That's normal. Stepping into your own identity can be scary, especially when you've spent so much of your life trying to fit into someone else's version of you. Give yourself the permission the younger you needed to explore who you are as an individual.

Start small. Say 'yes' to the opportunities that excite you, even if they feel risky. Speak up in the moment, even if your voice shakes. I don't mean you should feel tense or argue; rather, gently but firmly create boundaries, take up space and be yourself while trying out some of the following strategies:

- **Speak your mind:** Share your thoughts even if they're uncomfortable. You can say you 'feel something is important' without fear.

- **Say 'yes' to new opportunities:** Even if it scares you, take a chance. Growth happens when you step out of your comfort zone.
- **Set boundaries kindly:** It's okay to say 'no' or that you 'need some time for yourself right now'.
- **Celebrate your wins:** Don't downplay your achievements. Be proud of yourself!
- **Own your space:** Sit or stand comfortably, take up space and don't shrink yourself for others.
- **Speak up in conversations:** Your voice matters. Don't be afraid to share your opinion.
- **Ask for help when needed:** Don't hesitate to say you 'need support' when you do.
- **Prioritise your well-being:** Take time for your mental and physical health. You deserve it.
- **Ask for what you want:** If there's something you need or desire, ask for it. It could be a small favour or a big change – either way, your needs matter.
- **Take a stand for yourself:** If something doesn't feel right, speak up gently, even if it feels uncomfortable. 'I'm not okay with this' can be enough.
- **Allow yourself rest:** It's okay to say 'yes' to rest and recharge, even if you feel guilty. You need it to show up fully for yourself and others.

Use the 'Support circle' exercise below to help you get comfortable with sometimes choosing yourself.

Exercise: Support circle

Every time you choose yourself, you're sending a message. You're saying, 'I matter, my dreams matter and my life matters.' But when you start living as your true self, you might worry about how it will affect your relationships. Will your family still accept you? Will they see it as a rejection of everything they've given you?

These fears are real, because there's potentially lots at stake, so it's important to do this work in a safe way. Therefore, as a therapist, I encourage you not to do this alone, and to remember that not everything you do needs to be shared with family members who might not truly understand. An example is gentle boundaries. Not every boundary needs to be said out loud; some things you can just do gently for yourself, or you can simply appreciate how you gently show up for yourself.

Follow the steps below to explore this further:

1. **Acknowledge your fear of rejection:** Start by taking a few deep breaths. Write down the specific fears or concerns you have about family rejection. For example, 'They might think I'm being selfish' or 'They might stop supporting me'. Let yourself feel those fears without judgement.
2. **Identify your values and needs:** Write down what living as your authentic self means to you. What are the values or needs you're trying to honour? For example, 'I need to feel heard and respected' or 'I deserve to live without guilt.' Understanding your core values helps you stay grounded when facing rejection.
3. **Build your support circle:** Think about people in your life who can support you during this process. These could include a close friend, a mentor or a therapist. Write down their names and reach out to them for support, because you shouldn't have to do this alone. Even if they can't fully understand, their presence and encouragement will make a big difference.
4. **Reflect on rejection:** Imagine that a family member rejects your growth or changes. Write down how that feels and what your inner dialogue says. Then rewrite it with compassion: 'I know this is hard for them and my worth is not tied to just their approval. I am allowed to change and grow.'
5. **Take action:** Choose one person from your support circle and share your fears and thoughts with them. Tell them what you're working on and how they can support you. Knowing you're not alone will help you feel stronger and more grounded.

Sometimes, you might think you need to be loud about healing and growing, but that's far from the truth when you start this work. What you need to do is first hear yourself loudly and comfortably and feel safe within yourself. Take breaks when you need to.

The process of healing also requires support from others who understand and can hold space for your growth, so reach out to a trusted friend, family member, support group or therapist. Share your fears, your goals and your process with them. Ask them to check in on you regularly or to be there when you need a boost of encouragement. Having someone to lean on will help you feel less isolated and more empowered.

Setting boundaries

I want to introduce you to the concept of setting gentle boundaries. Instead of viewing boundaries as a means of breaking relationships, it's important to see them as a way to *maintain healthy relationships*. There's a misconception that only certain people are entitled to set boundaries, but boundaries are for everyone. This includes children and young people, who should be encouraged to express their needs and preferences because it will teach them how to create safety for themselves.

As an adult, it's important you use your voice and communicate what you're comfortable with and how you want to be treated. This process might initially feel daunting, particularly after all the conditioning you've experienced, but it's a crucial aspect of prioritising your own well-being.

Start by identifying your personal boundaries: the spaces you allow yourself to be in, the conversations you participate in and how you navigate your emotions. Reflect on the mental discipline you practice and identify any boundaries you may be overstepping. For example, you might find you're constantly worrying about upsetting others and, as a result, you end up neglecting your own needs. By doing so, you may be breaching your own boundaries and losing yourself in the process.

Understanding your personal boundaries will enable you to develop a healthy relationship with yourself, which in turn is necessary to engage with others in harmony. For instance, if a friend invites you to meet up but it's not feasible for you at that time, it's completely acceptable to express gratitude for the invitation and propose an alternative day that works better for you. Establishing and upholding your boundaries while also nurturing a compassionate relationship with yourself, and then extending that same compassion to others, will allow you to maintain the relationship.

Boundaries are not about imposing your beliefs on others or controlling them. They're about maintaining healthy relationships and self-respect, and about establishing and communicating your personal limits in a caring and respectful manner. The 'Gentle boundary' exercise on the next page will allow you to take the first steps towards setting and maintaining boundaries effectively.

Exercise: Gentle boundary 🧩

If setting boundaries feels too big, too scary or too 'rude', start small. This week, choose *one area* where you usually say 'yes', even when you don't want to. It could be one of the following:

- Picking up a call when you're emotionally drained
- Sitting through a conversation that makes you uncomfortable
- Agreeing to something out of guilt, not willingness

Now, instead of saying 'yes' automatically, try one of these soft responses:

- 'Can I let you know in a bit?'
- 'I'm a little tired right now – maybe another time?'
- 'I hear you. . . but I need to think about that.'

Write down one sentence you feel *comfortable enough* to say. Practise it in front of a mirror or with a trusted friend.

Why this matters: Small shifts build your boundary muscle. You're not being disrespectful; you're learning to honour both yourself *and* the relationship. Even a pause – even saying, 'Let me get back to you' – is a boundary.

COMMUNICATING YOUR BOUNDARIES TO YOUR PARENTS

Building understanding and acceptance with your parents isn't something that happens overnight. It's a process – one that often requires patience and empathy on both sides. These conversations aren't just about you expressing your feelings; they're also about creating a safe space where their fears and uncertainties can be gently acknowledged. It may take multiple discussions to plant the seeds of mutual respect and, even then, progress can feel slow. But *you* are initiating a safe conversation; *you* are in control of yourself here.

Sometimes, however, despite your best efforts and countless conversations, your parents may still not agree with or support the decisions you wish to make. This can leave you with a tough choice. Can you move forward with your decision, knowing they might not fully understand or accept it? Or do you step back and make a different choice to preserve that sense of harmony with them?

Neither option is easy, and both require courage, but whatever path you choose, remember that it doesn't diminish the love or respect you hold for your parents or the bravery it takes to carve out your own life. You're allowed to prioritise your growth while still cherishing your connection with them.

When engaging in conversations with your parents about your desires for certain boundaries, it's important to create an environment for open communication in which you can both consider their points of view and express your own needs. When you feel apprehensive about initiating a conversation, the uncertainty of the outcome can lead to heightened anxiety. This fear can significantly influence the tone and your choice of words during the conversation, so pay close attention to these factors as they can significantly impact the conversation.

Noticing even the smallest hint of discomfort or rejection on your parents' faces can feel deeply discouraging. It's natural to feel frustrated, but sometimes you have to separate yourself from the emotion and trust the way you're conveying the message. It's important to remember that your life experiences are vastly different from theirs. The lens through which they see the world has been shaped by their own struggles, values and upbringing, which can make it hard for them to fully grasp the weight of your words, the choices you're trying to make and the boundaries you're trying to create.

The 'Having constructive conversations with your parents' exercise below provides a framework through which you can approach these issues.

Exercise: Having constructive conversations with your parents

Getting started is never easy, but this framework will help you initiate a discussion with your parents. Here, I've given you some examples of what you can say, but feel free to adapt them so they feel authentic to you:

1. **Acknowledge your parents**
    - Begin by recognising their perspectives and feelings. This shows respect and helps set a positive tone for the conversation.

- Example: 'Mum, I wanted to talk to you about something important. I would really value your thoughts on this.'

2. **Acknowledge yourself**
    - Share your feelings honestly. Let them know that you're feeling nervous or uncertain about the conversation.
    - Example: 'I'm a bit nervous about sharing this with you, but I feel it's important.'

3. **Make space for the discussion**
    - Create an open environment for dialogue. Encourage them to express their thoughts while also making space for your perspective.
    - Example: 'I know this might be scary for you, and I'm scared too, but I don't want fear to stop us from trying something new together.'

4. **If the conversation becomes heightened, stop**
    - If you notice emotions rising, take a step back. Suggest pausing the conversation to allow everyone to regain their composure.
    - Example: 'I can sense we're getting a bit heated. Let's take a moment and come back to this in a little while.'

Have a look at my suggested starter sentences for the first two points: 'Mum, I wanted to talk to you about something important. I would really value your thoughts on this' and 'I'm a bit nervous about sharing this with you, but I feel it's important.' With both examples, you'll see that I've made space for your mother by addressing her directly and using 'you', but I've also made space for you by using 'I' statements. Remember, the moment you feel like there's too much discomfort, step out of the conversation and go back to it when you're both calm again.

Fear of change

Change, especially when it comes to making significant decisions or doing things differently, can be frightening, but – and I think this will resonate with you and be something your parents can relate to as well – when your parents emigrated, it was a monumental change for them. They left their families behind, stepped away from the culture they knew and arrived in a place that was often vastly different. They faced an avalanche of fear and uncertainty, not knowing what the future would hold, yet they did it anyway.

While their journey may not mirror yours exactly, the underlying emotions are similar. They, too, were stepping into the unknown, taking risks that deviated from what had come before. Anything you choose to do that feels different from their experiences will likely evoke fear in them as well, but here's the silver lining: as they start to see you navigating these changes and managing them, their trust in you will begin to build. They'll slowly start to feel more confident and reassured about your decisions, and this gradual shift can open up new avenues of connection between you.

So, when you're speaking with your parents about your own journey, remember this shared history. Acknowledge their fears and remind them you're not acting recklessly; you're forging your own path, just as they did. This connection to their past can help ease their worries and create a space where open dialogue can flourish. It's all about understanding and empathy, both for yourself and for them, as you navigate the complexities of change together. 'The blame-to-boundary transition' exercise below provides a framework to explore these concepts.

Exercise: The blame-to-boundary transition

This exercise will help you transform blame into actionable boundaries, with a focus on protecting yourself moving forward rather than being stuck in the past:

1. Identify a situation where you feel stuck in blame. For example, *I blame my family for making me feel unheard.*

2. Ask yourself what you need to protect yourself from feeling this way again. For example, *I need to set clear boundaries when discussing emotional topics so I don't feel dismissed.*

3. Write down a boundary to address the issue. For example, *I will only engage in conversations where I feel respected, and I'll walk away if that respect isn't there.*

4. Implement this boundary in real life. Then reflect on what that was like for you.

Many of us were never taught how to process difficult emotions like anger, betrayal or sadness, so blaming others feels like the most accessible option. However, as I ponder the word 'blame', I can't help but think about how much of our energy gets tied up in dwelling on our past experiences and feeling resentful towards those who may have contributed to our hardships. As I've said, it's easy to get stuck in that cycle of blame, but what next? Does it end with assigning blame?

Of course you should acknowledge that what you've been through was unfair and should never have happened, but to break this cycle, create a more fulfilling life and prevent passing this burden on to the next generation, it's crucial to actively build self-awareness, address generational trauma and consciously learn to allow yourself to want more for yourself. It's a challenging journey, but it's necessary to create a healthier and more supportive environment for yourself. When blame takes over, when stuckness takes over, it's almost like you're giving up on your future. Younger you needed support, needed someone to lean on. Now you can provide that support for yourself, which is what the 'Inner child healing box' exercise below represents.

Exercise: Inner child healing box

This is a tangible, creative way of providing comfort and reassurance to your inner child through symbolic items. This activity works because it combines creativity with emotional grounding, providing a physical reminder of your relationship with your inner child and offering reassurance during tough times.

1. **Find a small box or container and decorate it in a way that feels meaningful to you.** Use colours, patterns or symbols that connect to your childhood.

2. **Fill the box with items that represent safety, love and joy for your inner child.** For example:
   - A photo of yourself as a child to remind you of who you're nurturing;

- A comforting object like a small plush toy, a trinket from your childhood or even a handwritten note, perhaps describing a memory of something you loved as a child;
- Affirmations on slips of paper, such as 'You are safe' or 'You are loved and protected.'

3. **Open the box and connect with these items whenever you feel overwhelmed, neglected or self-critical.** Use this process as a reminder of the promise you've made to show up for your inner child.

Moving beyond blame doesn't mean ignoring the hurt or pretending everything's okay. It's about recognising that holding on to blame keeps you tied to the pain caused by others. Blame feels like a way to validate your experiences, but staying in that space can inhibit growth, self-discovery and joy and stop you from fully stepping into your healing.

Blame feels powerful at first, especially if you've spent years being silenced or dismissed. It can feel like reclaiming your voice, and that's an important part of the process, but healing asks for more. It asks you to look inward, focus on what *you* need to feel whole again - regardless of whether the people who hurt you apologise, change or even acknowledge their actions - and take back your power.

For many Brown women, this can feel especially hard, because the people we blame are often those closest to us - our parents, siblings or even partners. It's complex, because you may love these people and still feel deeply hurt by them, but moving beyond blame doesn't mean excusing their actions or letting them off the hook. It means releasing their control over your emotional state and choosing peace for yourself.

Moving beyond blame is also an act of self-love. When you let go of the idea that your healing depends on someone else's actions, you reclaim your energy and redirect it towards yourself. You give yourself permission to prioritise your growth, your peace and your future.

It's not what you say; it's how you say it

Whether it's with our parents, partners, friends or colleagues, we're constantly engaged in various forms of communication. However, the art of effective communication is often overlooked in our education and upbringing. It's not that people don't express themselves - they do -

but what matters are the nuances of how we convey our messages, the substance of what we communicate, the timing of our expressions and the intended audience. Merely repeating the same message without considering the manner in which it's delivered can judge the communication ineffective.

When engaging in conversations, you need to take into account the perspectives of the individuals involved and the context in which the communication is taking place. Each person's unique background, experiences and personal challenges shape how they perceive and respond to information. Therefore, it's necessary to be mindful of your audience and tailor your communications to resonate with them.

Every conversation is an opportunity to nurture a relationship with another individual, so it's important to recognise that it's not solely about our own expression. Instead, it's about creating a shared space where both parties can engage meaningfully. For example, when we think about speaking to our parents, we already know that there are certain things they'll easily grasp and others they might struggle to understand. This often comes from their habitual ways of doing things, shaped by their own experiences and upbringing.

If you're trying to discuss boundaries, you might need to recognise that your parents may not fully comprehend what boundaries are. To them, the concept might feel foreign or come across as aggressive or disrespectful. This can lead to misunderstandings, which is why it's so important to approach the conversation thoughtfully. The 'Translate your truth with care' exercise below gives you some pointers on how to approach these conversations.

Exercise: Translate your truth with care

Sometimes, the biggest challenge isn't knowing *what* you want to say – it's figuring out *how* to say it in a way that doesn't shut the other person down. This exercise will help you say hard things gently, especially in emotionally charged relationships.

1. Write down something you want to say to a loved one that feels difficult, even if you're not ready to say it out loud. Choose something real, like the following examples:
   - 'I need you to stop commenting on my body.'

- 'When you compare me to others, it hurts.'
- 'I feel alone in this family.'

2. Now, imagine you're translating that sentence for someone who *genuinely wants to understand you* but speaks a different emotional language. Rewrite the sentence to reflect care, not just frustration. You're still being honest – just with more intention. For example:
   - 'When you talk about my body, it makes me feel small and uncomfortable. I know that might not be your intention, but I'm asking you to stop.'
   - 'It's hard for me when you compare me to others. I really want to feel accepted as I am.'

3. Ask yourself: *Does this version honour what I feel* **and** *invite a real conversation?* If yes, hold onto it. Practise saying it to yourself. When the moment comes, you'll be ready.

Language lessons

Earlier, I mentioned the need to be mindful of your audience in any form of communication. When you're setting boundaries with your parents, you'll need to think about the language you're using and communicate in a way that resonates with their understanding. This doesn't necessarily mean speaking in your mother tongue, though that can be helpful. It's more about finding the right words and examples that bridge the gap between your perspective and theirs.

Consider giving them a relatable example – something they've experienced themselves. For instance, you might recall a time when your mum set a boundary, perhaps without even realising it. Maybe there was a situation where she said 'no' to someone asking for a favour that stretched her too thin. You could frame it as, 'Remember that time you told Auntie you couldn't help with her garden because you needed to rest? That was you setting a boundary.' That way, you're not just defining the term but showing how it applies to their own life, making it easier for them to understand.

By relating the concepts you want to discuss back to your parents' experiences, you help them see boundaries not as something foreign or aggressive but as a natural part of healthy relationships. This approach promotes dialogue rather than confrontation, allowing for a more constructive conversation. It's about meeting them where they are while gently guiding them towards new ideas.

Again, remember that it's a process. Change doesn't happen overnight, and it's okay if they don't fully get it right away. The important thing is that you're opening up the lines of communication and creating a space for understanding. By doing so, you're not just advocating for your own needs; you're also helping your parents expand their perspective, paving the way for deeper connections in the future.

When you're communicating with your parents and it leads to arguments or heightened tension, you need to recognise that this isn't just about the current conversation. It's a culmination of all those layers of built-up resentment, annoyance and irritability that you've been carrying from past interactions. Those feelings can seep into your tone and body language, turning what could be a constructive discussion into a heated exchange. You might find that even if your parents don't say anything overtly dismissive, a simple misunderstanding can trigger you. It's like a switch flips and suddenly you're thinking, *My parents don't understand me*. When that happens, your frustration takes over and, instead of expressing your needs calmly, you end up communicating from a place of irritability. That's when your boundaries are less likely to be noticed and respected.

Think of a moment when you tried to assert a boundary but felt ignored. That frustration can bubble up, right? You remember the tension in your voice and how your body felt awkward and stiff, maybe even closed off. If you use that frustrated tone every time you try to set a boundary, it's not surprising if the conversation doesn't go the way you hoped.

So, I encourage you to practice setting gentle boundaries, boundaries that come from a place of calmness and understanding (*see* pp. 167–71). This means creating space not just for *your* feelings but for theirs as well. It's about removing yourself from the heat of the moment. If you start to feel tense or recognise that you're triggered, take a step back. Breathe. Ground yourself. This pause can help you approach the conversation from a clearer, more centred place.

By doing this, you create an environment where your message can land more effectively. When you communicate from a space of calm, your parents are more likely to receive what you're saying without the added layers of defensiveness or misunderstanding. This gentle approach can transform the dialogue, allowing you to express your needs while also creating a more compassionate connection. Remember, it's all about progress, not perfection. Taking these small steps can lead to more meaningful conversations and a healthier dynamic in the long run.

The 'Recognising your triggers' exercise below is designed to help you build self-awareness and recognise your emotional state *before* speaking.

Exercise: Recognising your triggers

Sometimes, you only realise you're triggered *after* you've reacted. This visual tool helps you *catch it earlier*.

Draw a simple temperature meter, from 'cool' (0) to 'boiling' (10). Label it like this:

- 0–3: Calm: I can express myself with clarity.
- 4–6: Stirred: I feel tension rising, but I can pause.
- 7–10: Heated: I'm likely to react, not respond.

Before any tough conversation with your parents, ask yourself: *Where am I on this scale right now?* If you're above a 6, pause. Do something grounding, drink some water, walk, breathe and come back later.

What if the answer is 'no'?

One of the hardest truths to come to terms with is that your parents might say no. They might resist, question or simply misunderstand you. And then what? Does their resistance mean you can no longer live for yourself? Does it mean your voice no longer matters? These are heavy questions that often keep us paralysed in fear, stuck in a place where our needs and truths remain unspoken.

So many Brown women have confided in me, saying, 'I was terrified to bring this up with my dad' or 'I couldn't even imagine my mother understanding where I was coming from.' But then they took the step. They found the courage to speak their truth. And, to their surprise, they were met with agreement or, at the very least, a willingness to listen. It's not always the outcome they feared. Sometimes, the stories we tell ourselves about how others will react aren't rooted in reality; they're built on years of internalised fear, cultural conditioning and the avoidance of discomfort.

This isn't to say the outcome will always be perfect. Sometimes, despite your courage, the answer will still be 'no'. But it's not about the outcome. It's about the bravery it takes to show up for yourself. It's about overcoming the fear that's kept you silent for months, maybe even years. Having these conversations isn't just about trying to change someone's mind; it's about standing in your truth, advocating for yourself and giving yourself the permission to be heard. That, in itself, is a victory. Ask yourself this: are your conversations only about getting the other person to agree with you? Or can they be about something deeper: an opportunity to be understood, to connect, to break the silence that has weighed on you for so long? These conversations are as much about you as they are about the other person.

Remember, the beliefs we create about other people's reactions often come from our own fears, not their realities. The only way to truly know is to take that step, to have that conversation, to lean into the discomfort and to trust in your ability to handle whatever follows. Whether the response is understanding or resistance, you'll know you showed up for yourself – and that's where the real growth begins.

Case study

Amira opens up to her father

Amira, a 29-year-old British-Bangladeshi woman, came to therapy burdened and anxious. She talked about her home, growing up and how nothing was ever spoken about. Any tension or argument was brushed under the carpet, with everyone just acting like nothing happened. Recently, she met someone she's interested in, who she describes as kind, emotionally available and non-Bengali, but the thought of telling her father left her petrified.

In our sessions, she would often whisper, 'He's not going to understand. He'll think I've betrayed him. That I've forgotten who I am.'

We explored not just the fear of rejection but also generational expectations and what she'd learned growing up. Over time, Amira realised it wasn't just her father's reaction she feared; it was her own guilt. Her conditioning had convinced her that choosing love on her terms meant being ungrateful.

> Then, one day, she sat across from her dad at the dinner table and said, simply: *'There's someone in my life I'd like to tell you about.'*
> She expected silence. Anger. Dismissal.
> Instead, her father looked at her and said, *'If he respects you and you're happy, then I want to meet him.'*
> Amira wept in our next session. Not because it had all gone perfectly, but because she realised she'd been carrying a story in her head for years that no longer matched reality. Her father hadn't changed overnight, but he had listened. And that changed *everything*.

Don't forget about generational resilience

As a therapist, I often talk with clients about the emotional burdens and the pain handed down from family, friends and even society, but what I want you to realise is that, alongside the trauma, you've also inherited resilience. You might find yourself caught up and focused on what broke you, but I want to guide you to see what has built you, too. Resilience isn't always loud or visible, but it's there, quietly shaping you, giving you the strength to keep moving forward. Sometimes, I hear sentences like, 'If I have to go through that again I won't survive', but then they do – and they do.

When you think about your relationships, whether those with your parents, friends or others in your life, it's possible that some of those bonds have caused pain. Maybe your parents made decisions that were rooted in survival mode, decisions that felt harsh or unkind. Perhaps a close friend betrayed you or made you feel inadequate, and you carry the sting of that betrayal even now. But within those relationships, if you look closely, there were also lessons in resilience. You might not have felt it in the moment, but those experiences required you to adapt, to persevere, to survive.

Let's talk about family first. Your parents or grandparents might have lived through war, migration or systemic oppression. They might have parented you through the lens of their own unhealed wounds, projecting their anxieties or fears on to you. For instance, they might have been overly critical, believing that pushing you harder was the only way to secure your success. Or they might have silenced your feelings, not because they didn't care but because they didn't know how to process their own feelings. These dynamics can hurt deeply, but they also feed into resilience.

And what about friends? Perhaps you've experienced friendships that were filled with competition, gossip or judgement. Those relationships may have left you questioning your worth or feeling isolated. But even in those moments, you were learning. You learned what you didn't want in your friendships. You learned to recognise when someone wasn't safe or supportive. And you began to understand what healthy, nourishing connections should look like. Discovering your own needs and boundaries through the pain is resilience.

How about romantic partners? How do you know what you do and don't want unless you've had some difficult, perhaps painful, experiences? We tend to learn how to navigate things by experiencing or at least witnessing them. Blaming yourself because you made a mistake or didn't do something correctly doesn't sound fair – and doesn't take into account the lessons you took away.

Resilience isn't just about bouncing back, though. It's about moving forward with greater awareness. It's about recognising the strength that already exists within you, even if it feels buried under layers of hurt. When I say that resilience is in your DNA, I mean it quite literally. Science tells us that our bodies don't just carry trauma; they also carry the memory of survival. Your ancestors endured not just for themselves but for you. Their ability to adapt, to push forward despite the odds, is a gift they've passed down to you.

So, how do you connect with this resilience? Start by reflecting on the coping strategies you've seen in those around you. For example:

- How did your mother get through the hardest days? Was it through prayer, humour or a relentless drive to provide?
- How did your father keep going when the world seemed stacked against him? Did he lean on routines, community or sheer determination?
- And in friendships or wider social circles, what kept people together? Was it shared laughter, traditions or simply the knowledge that someone else was there?

Look at your own resilience. Think about the times you've felt broken or lost yet somehow found the strength to keep going. Maybe it was after a toxic friendship ended or when a family conflict left you questioning your place. How did you cope? What inner resources did you tap into?

Generational resilience is also deeply tied to community, especially in the South Asian experience. Think about the aunties who came together during times of crisis, offering meals or support even when they didn't have much themselves. Think about the uncles who worked multiple jobs to build a future for their families. Those acts of collective resilience are part of your story, too.

But resilience doesn't mean you have to carry the weight of others' expectations or sacrifice your happiness for their survival. This is where your generation has the opportunity to transform resilience into something even more powerful. You can honour the strength of those who came before you while creating space for your own healing and growth. You can say, 'I am grateful and sad for what they endured, and I don't have to endure the same.'

You are the product of generations of strength, love and survival. And as you walk your own path, remember that resilience isn't just about enduring hardship; it's about creating joy, finding peace and living a life that feels true to you. You carry the legacy of those who came before you, and you also have the power to build a new one.

Just forgive and forget!

Forgiveness is one of the most misunderstood parts of healing. Many of you grew up in a culture where forgiveness was framed as a duty – a moral obligation tied to being a 'good' daughter, a 'respectful' child or a 'kind' person. Forgiveness is often conflated with forgetting, brushing things under the carpet or reconciling with those who hurt you. You might have been told, 'They're your family – just let it go', but this version of forgiveness can feel invalidating, as though your pain and experiences don't matter.

True forgiveness, however, isn't about forgetting what happened or pretending the hurt isn't there. It's also not about forcing a reconciliation with someone who refuses to accept accountability or change their behaviour. Forgiveness, at its core, is a deeply personal choice. It's not about the other person; it's about you. It's about deciding that you no longer want the actions of others to hold power over your emotional well-being. It's about freeing yourself from the resentment that weighs you down, even when the people who hurt you may never fully understand the impact of their actions.

Forgiveness doesn't mean the hurt goes away instantly or that you're okay with what happened. You don't have to let it go in a way that minimises your pain. Instead, think of forgiveness as releasing yourself from the need for someone else to 'fix' what they broke. It's saying to yourself, *I won't let this hold me back any more, even if they never apologise, even if they don't change.* It's an act of self-care, not self-sacrifice.

There's also no timeline for forgiveness. Maybe you're not ready, and that's okay. It's a process that unfolds as you work through it. I also want to say, though, that some of you may not forgive. In fact, it might help you stay true to yourself as a reminder. What do I mean? Well, many survivors choose not to forgive, because this choice might help to fuel their purpose in life. I understand that. Ultimately, what's important is that whether to forgive or not is your choice, one that comes from a place of self-awareness and empowerment rather than cultural pressure or guilt.

Forgiveness often gets tangled up with forgetting and reconciliation, but they are not the same. Forgetting implies erasing the pain, but trauma doesn't work like that. Your experiences shape you, and pretending something didn't happen only suppresses your healing. You might think, *Why would I forget? It helped me reassess my boundaries.* Absolutely!

Reconciliation, on the other hand, is a two-way street. It requires the other person to take responsibility, show genuine remorse and work towards rebuilding trust. You can forgive someone without reconciling with them. Reconciliation depends on the other person's actions. Forgiveness is your choice.

In a journal, answer the following questions, then revisit your answers every so often to see if your views have changed. If they have changed, answer the questions again:

- What does forgiveness mean to me?
- Why do I want to forgive?
- Why do I choose not to forgive?

Use the 'Redefining forgiveness for yourself' exercise below to explore what the concept means to you.

Exercise: Redefining forgiveness for yourself

Take a quiet moment to sit with the word *forgiveness*. Let go of the version that was passed down to you – the one that asked you to stay silent, to suppress your truth, to be the 'bigger person'.

Now answer these prompts in writing, without censoring yourself:

- When I hear the word *forgiveness*, what emotions come up for me?
- Who have I felt pressured to forgive, and how did that pressure feel in my body?
- What would forgiveness look like if it centred my healing instead of someone else's comfort?
- If I chose *not* to forgive, would that be a decision rooted in pain or in self-honour?
- What am I still holding on to and what would it feel like to release *just a little bit* of that today?

This exercise isn't about forcing a decision; it's about becoming honest with yourself. You can come back to these questions over time as your feelings evolve.

Case study

Jasmine's journey to rebuilding relationships

Jasmine, 31, had carried resentment towards her parents for years, feeling burdened by their expectations. As an adult, she realised that holding on to anger was preventing her from growing. Letting go felt overwhelming, but instead of expecting an instant fix, Jasmine took small steps. She began by acknowledging her feelings without judgement and setting small boundaries to protect her peace. Over time, she reframed her thoughts, realising that forgiveness wasn't about excusing the past but freeing herself from it. By taking these intentional steps, Jasmine started rebuilding a healthier, more understanding relationship with her parents.

Beyond external validation

For so many of us, healing often feels tied to something external – an apology, an acknowledgement or a sign that the people who hurt us understand the pain they caused. It's natural to crave this. When you grew up in a family or community where emotional needs were dismissed, the idea of someone finally seeing and validating your pain can feel like the missing piece in your healing. So much of that is normal. As humans, it's part of who we are, but wanting that validation and waiting for that moment can leave you stuck.

The hard truth is that some apologies will never come. Some people may never acknowledge the harm they've caused, whether because they lack the emotional capacity, the awareness or even the willingness to reflect on their actions, but it's emotionally so draining trying to get someone to understand your view when they can't see it through your lens. They can only see themselves.

This is where healing beyond external validation becomes a radical and necessary act. It means letting go of the need for someone else to say, 'I'm sorry for hurting you.' It's about recognising that their inability to offer you closure doesn't mean you can't move forwards. Do you really need someone else to give you closure? It's about understanding that your healing is yours to claim, not theirs to grant.

Validation begins with you. Instead of focusing on what others should have done, focus on what you can do now. Acknowledge your emotions, accept your story and remind yourself that your worth was never tied to their ability to do right by you. Healing isn't about waiting for others to change. Emotional independence is the process of reclaiming your sense of self, separate from how others treat you. It's recognising that while other people's actions may have shaped your past, they do not have to define your future. Does that mean people can treat you however they want? Of course not, because you will not allow it.

Emotional independence begins with self-soothing. When you feel overwhelmed, instead of waiting for someone to comfort you, ask yourself, *What do I need right now? How can I get this? What spaces feel safe for me?* That doesn't mean you can't ask for help from others, though. While it's important to learn how to regulate yourself, it's just as important to build your support networks and sense of self.

Building emotional independence doesn't mean shutting people out or pretending you don't need connection. It means learning to differentiate between healthy interdependence and emotional reliance. It's about taking ownership of your healing journey and saying to yourself, *I can move forward without the permission or understanding of those who have hurt me and not apologised.*

Breaking generational trauma isn't about blaming our families. Yes, it can feel like part of your healing process, but it doesn't stop there. It's about understanding what shaped them and what shaped us. The toxic behaviours you may have witnessed at home – emotional neglect, silence around pain, constant conflict or being made to shrink yourself – didn't start with you. They often began generations ago, but just because you grew up in dysfunction doesn't mean you're doomed to live in it forever. You have the power to build awareness, to pause, to choose differently.

Healing isn't about having a perfect life. It's about slowly, gently creating a life that feels more honest, more whole and more loving than the one you came from. And you deserve that. You always have.

5. Mental health

In our community, mental health is an unspoken narrative, a hushed conversation behind closed doors. We learn early on that struggles of the mind are a private affair, something to be managed silently or, worse, denied entirely. There's a persistent belief in South Asian culture that seeking help or even naming the struggle is a sign of failure and a crack in the perfect facade we've been taught to uphold. But how long can we carry the weight of silence before it becomes too much to bear?

If you've ever felt like your pain is invisible, your feelings don't belong or you're screaming internally while the world moves on around you, this chapter is for you. If you've ever been told to 'snap out of it' or that your struggles are 'just a phase', or if you've been made to feel weak for wanting to reach out for help, I see you. And I want you to know you're not alone in this.

Struggles with mental health are not a failure or a flaw. They're shaped by the stories we've inherited, the environments we grew up in and the expectations we've carried, often without even realising it. This chapter is about breaking down the stigmas that surround mental health in our community, but also about recognising how these narratives have shaped us and, most importantly, how we can rewrite them.

This chapter is also an invitation to breathe, to reflect and to begin unlearning the shame that surrounds mental health issues. It's a space to acknowledge the ways in which we've been hurt by silence and stigma, but also a space to find hope. Together, we'll confront and debunk the myths we've been told: that marriage, children or strict environments can 'fix' mental health struggles. We'll talk about what healing really looks like and how it begins when we choose to value our well-being as much as we've been taught to value others' opinions – and how we can value our mental health just as we've learned to look after our physical health. Your mind and body are interconnected, and if you ignore your mental health, it will show up in your physical health.

So, as we step into this conversation, I encourage you to hold compassion for yourself. Just as in the previous chapters, we're focusing on a heavy topic that may stir feelings you didn't realise were buried. That's okay; it's part of the process. Take a pause and come back if you need to, because your mental health really matters. And, as we navigate this chapter, know that you're not walking this path alone.

The Traditional Narrative

How was mental health talked about when you were growing up? What words were used? What kind of tone was employed? What views did you internalise, and how much have those views changed? Was it even discussed? Sit with your reflections for a moment.

When we talk about mental health in the South Asian community, we're not just talking about diagnosed conditions like anxiety or depression; we're talking about the everyday emotional struggles that so many of us carry in silence. Being low, having a bad day, feeling overwhelmed, burned out, stuck or numb – these are all part of our mental health. So too is childhood trauma, heartbreak, postpartum depression, self-doubt, addiction, grief and the exhaustion that comes from constantly trying to be everything for everyone.

Yet in many of our homes, there's little space to say, 'I'm not okay.' Speaking up about your mental health, going to therapy, setting boundaries – these things can be misunderstood, judged or seen as weakness. Many of us were raised to stay quiet, to push through, to be strong no matter what. If mental health was mentioned, you might have been given advice that at the time didn't feel particularly helpful, to say the least. For example, perhaps you were told any or all of the following:

- 'Don't be depressed.'
- 'You shouldn't be stressed.'
- 'It will pass.'
- 'We had it worse.'
- 'You need to be stronger.'
- 'Go pray.'
- 'Stop seeking attention.'

In the Brown community, mental health is equated with being unstable, dangerous or incapable of functioning in society. Words like 'crazy' are thrown around dismissively, as though struggling mentally is something shameful or even contagious. If someone has poor mental health, you may have been warned to stay away from them. It's this narrative that silences so many of us, holding us back from being open about any struggles we might have with our mental health.

For Brown women, this stigma cuts especially deep. We're told to keep quiet, endure and never let our struggles show because they could threaten our family's reputation. As we've seen in previous chapters, it's about staying quiet and keeping up appearances.

Have you ever hesitated to admit that you felt anxious, overwhelmed or depressed because you were afraid of the reaction? Maybe you've heard someone in your family say, 'She's just overthinking it – it's nothing serious' or 'Mental health issues are for people who are weak.' Perhaps you've even convinced yourself to *just get over it*, because the alternative – acknowledging your pain – feels like opening Pandora's box. This is the narrative so many of us have been handed: that only 'crazy' people struggle with their mental health.

And what happens when this belief takes root? It creates fear. You become terrified of being labelled or judged. Maybe you've seen how others in your family or community have been whispered about, pitied or avoided entirely. You might worry that people will see you differently, that you'll be defined by your struggle and not by the fullness of who you are.

As Brown women, you're taught to keep everything 'together', to be the glue that holds the family, marriage and community in place. The idea of showing vulnerability or admitting that you're struggling feels like you aren't good enough or have failed. People might reject you for your struggles, because these things weigh heavily on women as you are meant to be 'strong'.

And then what happens when you internalise this fear? You start minimising your own struggles. You tell yourself, *It's not that bad* or *Other people have it worse*. You push yourself harder, keep smiling through the pain and bury your feelings so deeply that they begin to manifest in other ways. Physical symptoms like headaches, stomach aches and fatigue start showing up, but even then, you may have been told to 'Pray harder' or 'Just be grateful.' Your sleep is impacted; your appetite is impacted. So many different things show up; but you probably don't realise they're related.

This narrative doesn't just harm you; it isolates you. It forces you to carry your pain in silence, ashamed of something that is completely human. And it keeps you from seeking the support you need. It's a cycle of suppression that convinces us our struggles aren't real or valid unless they're visible or extreme.

Marriage – the ultimate fix

From a young age, Brown girls are told that marriage is the ultimate goal, the crown jewel of our existence, the moment when everything will finally fall into place. Then, if mental health struggles arise, this same narrative is weaponised against us: 'Once you get married, you'll feel better' or 'A husband will give you stability.' These are the messages that echo in countless Brown households, even when the reality couldn't be further from the truth.

Have you ever been told that your sadness, anxiety or exhaustion will simply vanish once you're married? Maybe you've heard it from family members who genuinely believe they're offering you a solution. Or maybe it's been framed as a warning: 'Don't let anyone know you're struggling or no one will want to marry you.' These words can feel like a slap in the face, reducing your very real pain to a 'problem' that marriage is expected to fix.

For many Brown women, the pressure to hide their struggles becomes overwhelming, because marriage isn't just about personal happiness - it's about family honour, societal approval and securing your place in the community. Many men will also relate to this, as parents see marriage to be the ultimate solution. Addiction? No problem, a woman can cure this. Going off the rails? Marriage will settle him down. 'Naughty'? Getting wed will sort that out. Meanwhile, all this will probably be hidden from the man's potential partner.

This belief that marriage will magically solve mental health struggles is deeply flawed, but it's rooted in the traditional narrative that a woman's worth is tied to her role as a wife. Struggles like anxiety or depression are dismissed as temporary hurdles, ones that can be smoothed over with a wedding ceremony. But what happens when the struggles remain or become even worse after marriage? What happens when the pressure to meet your husband's expectations or manage your in-laws' demands compound the very mental health challenges you were already carrying?

Many women end up feeling like an encumbrance being passed around, as though their parents are relieved the daughter with mental health problems isn't 'their responsibility' any more.

For so many women, this narrative that marriage will solve their mental health issues becomes a trap. They enter marriage believing it will bring relief, only to find that the burden of hiding their struggles intensifies. You might find yourself wondering why you still feel anxious, lonely or sad despite 'having it all' – a husband, a home, a family. The truth is, marriage isn't a cure. It's not a solution to mental health struggles, and nor should it be expected to be.

This pressure to hide mental health challenges in order to secure a good proposal creates a cycle of silence and shame. Families fear that if your struggles become known, you'll be deemed undesirable. So, instead of encouraging open conversations or seeking professional help, they push you to suppress your emotions and put on a brave face. But this silence comes at a cost. It not only prevents healing, but it also sets the stage for a life lived behind a mask, where your real self is buried beneath layers of societal expectations.

And let's talk about the emotional toll this takes. The weight of pretending to be okay, of constantly performing a version of yourself that feels acceptable to others, can be exhausting. It teaches you to prioritise appearances over your well-being, to sacrifice your own needs for the sake of preserving a family's image. But where does that leave you? How long can you carry this before it begins to break you?

The idea that marriage is the answer to mental health struggles places the responsibility for your well-being on an external factor, denying you the opportunity to truly heal and grow. And it perpetuates the stigma that mental health struggles are something to be ashamed of, something to be hidden rather than understood.

Where you may have dreamed of marriage as a new chapter for yourself, instead it can lead to deeply painful issues. Whether it's your relationship with your partner or your in-laws calling you crazy, it all becomes your fault. You wonder how you can keep your head above water.

By now, you'll recognise some of the patterns we've explored together throughout this book: secrecy, shame, the pressure to keep up appearances. These aren't just isolated issues; they form the emotional backdrop many of us were raised in, and they all deeply affect your mental health. When you grow up being told to stay quiet, to hide the messy parts of your life, to prioritise reputation over reality, you start to internalise that your feelings aren't valid or safe to express.

That constant emotional suppression builds up over time, showing up as anxiety, depression, burnout, disconnection or feeling like you're never enough. These conditions shape how you cope, how you relate to others and how you treat yourself, so when we talk about mental health, we have to talk about all of this, too.

> ### Being sent away
>
> Within the South Asian community, there's also the misguided belief that changing an individual's environment will 'fix' their mental health issues. For many families there was a period when this translated into sending children back to their home country or placing them in a stricter, more controlled setting. You might hear people say, 'A few months back home will sort you out', but, while being away and having a break can be healing, if you don't ask the person what happened, what they're struggling with and what they want, it won't work.
>
> This approach often does more harm than good. Imagine already feeling lost or misunderstood, only to be uprooted and placed in an unfamiliar environment. For some, being sent 'back home' means being separated from the support systems they've managed to build. This can leave individuals feeling abandoned, disconnected and even more isolated than before.
>
> The belief that stricter environments or cultural immersion will resolve mental health issues reflects a lack of understanding about what mental health actually entails. Struggles like anxiety, depression or trauma aren't about discipline or proximity to culture. They're deeply personal experiences that require care, empathy and, often, professional support. Sending someone 'back home' doesn't address the root causes of their pain; it merely shifts the problem to a new setting.

Having faith

I bet you've been told, 'Your faith is weak; just go and pray.' When I talk about mental health on social media, I still hear this. Maybe you've felt overwhelmed by anxiety, weighed down by depression or struggled with thoughts you don't fully understand. Instead of someone asking how they can help you or encouraging you to seek help, you've heard things like, 'It's probably the evil eye.' Maybe someone has suggested that you've been possessed by a jinn (in the Islamic context), a demon (in the context of Christianity) or any other evil spirit from your own religion, or perhaps they've said that your struggles are a result of losing touch with your faith. Your family may believe you're being punished for a lack of devotion, or you may have been taken to a religious healer or scholar instead of a doctor in the hope that prayers or rituals will resolve what you're going through.

And in those moments, you're left wondering if your pain is your fault, if you're somehow not doing enough to be okay. This is a narrative that so many of us in the South Asian community have grown up hearing. Mental health isn't seen for what it is. Instead, it's linked to your religion, as if it's your fault because you aren't doing enough.

If this has been your experience, it's important to know that it isn't because your family doesn't care. They do these things because, for generations, this is what people turned to when they didn't know what else to do. When mental health wasn't talked about and there weren't culturally informed therapists or resources available, families relied on what they knew, which was religion, spirituality and traditional beliefs. Turning to a religious scholar or healer felt like the best way to help, even though it often meant ignoring the deeper reasons behind someone's pain.

And what happens when the prayers and rituals don't work the way they expect them to? If you've ever been told that your mental health struggles are because of a lack of faith, I want you to know this: your pain is not a reflection of your worth or your spirituality. You are not struggling because you are weak or because you've done something wrong. Mental health challenges are not punishments or the result of you being a 'bad human'; they are human experiences, and they deserve to be treated with the same compassion as physical health issues.

I'm not saying that your faith or spirituality doesn't matter. In fact, it can be a beautiful source of strength and healing alongside professional help. Faith doesn't have to stand in opposition to professional help; you can hold space for both. You can pray, find comfort in your spiritual practices and also work with a therapist. It doesn't have to be one or the other.

In fact, I've worked with many, many clients who've been in a really dark place, and it's been faith that they've held on to, faith that has grounded them, alongside professional help from a therapist who is faith sensitive and culturally sensitive, and who understands the nuances. I'm not saying that faith should be ignored – absolutely not – but what I am saying is that poor mental health has nothing to do with weak faith. Let me share Ayesha's story with you (see below).

Case study

Ayesha's journey to therapy

Ayesha, a 29-year-old mother of two, sat nervously in her first therapy session. She smiled, yet I could see the exhaustion. Therapy was her secret. Not even her husband or parents knew. If they did, she feared being asked why she needed therapy and being told to 'just pray'.

Ayesha had been struggling with postpartum depression since the birth of her youngest child, now six months old. She often felt a sense of hopelessness she couldn't explain. She cried in the shower, snapped at her toddler over small things and sometimes lay awake, haunted by intrusive thoughts she dared not share with anyone. Thoughts like, *What if I hurt my baby?* or *What kind of mother am I to feel this way?* or *Do I even love my child?*

Her shame ran deep. In her family, mental health wasn't something anyone discussed openly. Growing up, she was told that faith was the answer to every problem. Whenever she expressed distress, elders reminded her to pray more, read religious texts or recite specific verses. Ayesha believed she was failing, not just as a mother but as a Muslim woman.

She would say things like, 'I feel like I'm disappointing God' and 'If I had stronger faith, I wouldn't need to be here.' In our sessions, Ayesha began to explore how cultural narratives had shaped her beliefs about strength and weakness. She realised that in her community, suffering in silence was often seen as a virtue, a sign of resilience. Therapy, on the other hand, felt like a symbol of failure.

I would gently challenge these thoughts and explore how faith and mental health could coexist. Ayesha reflected on how her spiritual practices had always been a source of comfort. Now she was losing the willpower to do anything.

> Ayesha's most troubling struggle was her intrusive thoughts. She worried she was a terrible mother for having them. We spoke about intrusive thoughts being a common symptom of postpartum depression and not reflecting a person's character or intentions. Slowly, Ayesha learned to separate herself from these thoughts, recognising them as part of her condition, not who she was.
>
> One day, she shared with her husband that she was attending therapy. To her surprise, he was supportive and realised that fear and shame were holding her back from sharing. Together, they decided not to tell extended family for now, recognising the stigma, but also prioritising Ayesha's well-being.
>
> Ayesha came to understand that seeking therapy didn't make her faith weaker. In fact, it strengthened it. By caring for her mental health, she was better able to fulfil her roles as a mother, wife and individual. She began to see therapy as part of her journey, not a departure from it.

Comparison culture

Have you ever been compared to someone else in your family or community? Maybe a cousin, neighbour or auntie's child? Perhaps some of these comments will sound familiar:

- 'Look at your cousin. She's married, has two kids and still manages a full-time job. Why can't you be more like her?'
- 'So-and-so's daughter just became a doctor. You're still figuring out what you want to do?'
- 'Your brother bought a house at 30. What are you doing with your life?'
- 'That family's daughter always makes time for his parents. You barely even call.'
- 'She lost all her baby weight so quickly – what's your excuse?'
- 'Your friend started her own business and you're still stuck in that job?'

Maybe you've overheard whisperings at family gatherings, such as praise for someone else's 'perfect' child while your own or your sibling's struggles were dismissed or gossiped about. These comments may come casually, even with a laugh, but they land heavily. They create unspoken standards that many of you feel pressured to meet, silently shaping how you see yourselves and what you believe you're worth.

Comparison is so common in South Asian culture, but it's rarely intentionally cruel. It's seen as a way of guiding or motivating, and it's so normal that no one gives much thought to the impact. Many parents believe that comparing you to someone else's child is just them pushing you, wanting you to do better, but they don't realise that, actually, they may be doing the opposite – because when you're the one being compared, it can feel anything but harmless.

The words may not come from a place of malice, but they might make you question yourself: *Am I really struggling or am I just being weak?* When it comes to your mental health, these things can have a profound effect on your confidence, your self-esteem and your self-worth, and they can create anxiety.

There's this idea that if someone else can do it, so can you, but mental health doesn't work like that. Comparing your struggles to someone else's struggles completely dismisses the unique circumstances, emotions and challenges that you face. It reduces something deeply personal to a competition, where you always seem to fall short.

This culture of judgement doesn't just come from others; it often seeps into how you view yourself. You might feel like you need to hide your struggles, put on a brave face and pretend everything's fine. You might tell yourself that you just need to push through, because admitting you're struggling feels like admitting defeat.

Dual identities

I believe many of you reading this now will be part of a second generation. If that's the case, you probably already know what it's like to live with expectations shaped on the one hand by the traditions and values of your parents' homeland, and on the other by the culture of the country you call home. This duality is both a privilege and a burden. It can give you a rich identity, but it also creates tension, especially when it comes to mental health.

When your parents left their home countries, often under difficult circumstances, in search of better opportunities, they probably had to enter survival mode. For them, enduring hardship wasn't a choice; it was a necessity. So, when they see you struggling it can be confusing, or they might feel it invalidates their own struggles. This may cause them to say things like, 'We didn't have these problems back home' or 'We went through so much and we didn't complain.'

But the challenges faced by second-generation children are different. You're not just navigating school, work and relationships; you're also balancing those two sets of expectations. At home, you're expected to uphold your family's values, traditions and dreams. Outside, you're expected to fit into a culture that often doesn't understand your background.

Perhaps you sometimes felt left out at school. You may have found it difficult to fit in at work. Depending on how diverse it was where you grew up and how many other Brown people there were, you may even have felt ashamed of who you are. And some of you may have experienced bullying and racism. It's exhausting to constantly shift between these identities, and it can leave you feeling like you don't fully belong in either world.

On top of this, there's the pressure to succeed, to make your parents' sacrifices worthwhile. Perhaps you've heard things like, 'We gave up everything for you' or 'You're our only hope.' These words can create a pressure that feels impossible to bear, even though you really try not to complain and do want to make them proud.

For some of you, your mental health struggles may be dismissed entirely, perhaps as a 'Western thing'. Your parents might suggest that you're lazy or lack gratitude, that you've been influenced by other people or that you're making things up. They might say, 'Back home, we didn't have depression or anxiety', but this isn't true. Mental health struggles have always existed – they just weren't talked about or understood in the same way. One statement I often hear is, 'This generation of kids are too weak', and it underlines to me how uninformed people still are and that they aren't familiar with the concept of generational trauma.

But let's pause for a moment and recognise this: the immigrant experience is complex. Your parents' dismissiveness or misunderstanding doesn't automatically mean they don't care about you. They're navigating their own fears, their own cultural conditioning and their own unspoken struggles. Comprehending this doesn't excuse the harm, but it helps us see the bigger picture.

Case study

Aaliya opens up

Aaliya, a 21-year-old Pakistani woman, came to therapy saying she didn't know what was wrong with her, only that she felt *empty*. She'd grown up in a traditional household where strength meant not showing vulnerability and pain was something you prayed through, not talked about. She was the middle child, the quiet one, the dependable one. No one in her family ever asked her how she was doing.

In our early sessions, Aaliya struggled to find the language for what she was feeling. She often described herself as lazy, distracted, or 'just not normal'. Her days were flat; she couldn't get out of bed on some mornings, and when she did, she felt like she was moving through the world with heaviness. She carried a deep guilt for not being able to 'just get on with it' like her parents had. Her father had once said, 'When we came here, we worked two jobs and never complained. What do you lot have to be sad about?' And Aaliya internalised that.

But underneath her numbness was a well of tears, years of suppressing herself, years of carrying her family's hopes while silently unravelling inside. Through therapy, she slowly began to realise that what she was feeling wasn't laziness – it was depression. Real, valid and painful.

The turning point came when she finally opened up to her mother. With a trembling voice, she said, 'Ammi [Mum], I don't think I'm okay. I feel like I'm breaking inside and I don't know why.' Her mother stared at her in stunned silence. Then, after a long pause, she softly replied, 'Beti [daughter], I used to feel like that too, but I didn't know what it was. I thought I was just tired.'

That conversation didn't fix everything, but it cracked something open, for both of them. Aaliya felt human. And for the first time, she felt seen not for what she did for others but for what she was going through inside. She decided to go to the doctor with her mum.

The therapy taboo

In the South Asian community, there's a taboo around getting professional help for your mental health. You've probably heard people say all sorts of negative things about therapy and therapists. As a result, you may feel embarrassed about wanting therapy or scared about accessing it.

However, it's heartbreaking to hear someone say, 'I've stopped myself from accessing therapy because my issue isn't that bad' – because how bad does it need to be for you to finally ask for support? No one is rewarding you for your suffering.

In lots of Brown families, seeking therapy is still seen as a last resort – something you do when things are completely unravelling – or worse, the ultimate admission of failure. If you've heard phrases like, 'Why would you share our family's problems with a stranger?' or 'We don't need therapy; we just need to pray harder', you're not alone. These beliefs are deeply rooted in generational patterns, where strength is equated with silence and vulnerability is mistaken for weakness.

Therapy has often been dismissed as unnecessary or even shameful in our community, because of the cultural stigma attached to mental health. There's a widespread fear that seeking help is a public announcement that something is fundamentally wrong with you. In a culture where reputation often feels like everything, this fear can silence people for years. It's not uncommon to hear elders say things like, 'People will think you're crazy', and that fear of being judged or ostracised can leave many of you with unacknowledged and unaddressed mental health issues.

I understand that you may have to overcome a lot of barriers to access therapy. Assuming you know how to access it in the first place, you may be concerned that someone will recognise you as you're going into the therapist's office – even if the therapy is held at the doctor's surgery, so you might be able to explain it away as an acceptable doctor's appointment. You may worry that a therapist won't understand your culture and will be judgemental. You may be afraid of a diagnosis, because you think the therapist might also think you're 'crazy'.

And then there's the issue of trust. Perhaps you're worried about what might happen if the confidentiality of therapy is breached. In small South Asian circles, where everyone seems to know everyone else, the idea of opening up to a therapist may feel like a gamble: *What if they know someone in my family?*

These are all valid fears, shaped by a culture that has long prioritised privacy and caution over openness and healing. However, professional support can help you work through the things you're struggling with and give you tools and tips that will help you manage. But, when therapy is viewed as taboo, it denies you the opportunity to heal, grow and break the cycles of pain that have been passed down for generations.

Suicide and self-harm

This is an extremely sensitive subject, and you may find this difficult, but I want you to think about how often you've heard anyone in your family or community talk about suicide. Most of the time, you won't hear it being spoken about openly, yet I can give you countless cases of suicide within our community. The misconception is that if you speak about it, 'they'll do it', but the fact is, when you talk about it, you create a safe space where individuals don't feel shameful about seeking help.

Think about self-harm and, if it's spoken about at all, the way in which it's talked about. So often, people dismiss it with comments like, 'She's just being attention-seeking.' I really don't like the term 'attention-seeking' because it's used in such a negative way, but if we really paid attention to the phrase, we might understand that, yes, they are struggling with their mental health and are therefore seeking attention; they are asking for support. However, because of the shame, they can't verbalise it, and the only way they feel they can express their pain is by harming themselves. Of course, I appreciate that this is a simplification of why people self-harm, but there is also truth in it.

The case study below explores these topics further.

Case study

Priya finds space to talk about the loss of her sister

Priya, a 28-year-old Indian woman, came to therapy one year after losing her younger sister, Anjali, to suicide. Anjali had been only 20.

Priya said in our session, 'She didn't talk much, stayed in her room, kept to herself. We just thought that was her personality: shy, private, not like me.'

But after Anjali's death, everything Priya thought she'd understood about her sister shifted. She began remembering the little things: how Anjali would sleep all day, how she avoided eye contact, how she once said, 'I don't think I fit anywhere.' At the time, Priya didn't know how to respond. No one in their family ever talked about mental health. Struggling was seen as weakness.

'I wish I'd asked more questions,' Priya whispered in one of our early sessions. 'I wish I'd known that silence can be a scream.'

> In therapy, she worked through her grief and guilt. But she also found a sense of purpose – to speak more openly about suicide, to create conversations her family never had.
>
> This is why I speak so openly about these topics. Because for every Anjali, there are so many others who are struggling silently, quietly slipping away under the radar of cultural expectations and misunderstood behaviours. And for every Priya, there's a loved one left behind, trying to piece together a puzzle with missing pieces, trying to understand something that was never explained to them in the first place.

Mental health isn't always loud. It doesn't always look like crying or dramatic changes. Sometimes, it's the absence of presence. The withdrawal, the stillness, the smile that doesn't quite reach the eyes. And in cultures like ours, where being 'strong' is praised and vulnerability is rarely modelled, it becomes even harder to notice. Let's build families and communities where silence doesn't become a death sentence. Where asking for help isn't a betrayal of strength but a testament to it. Where we don't wait until it's too late to start having these conversations.

Let's move now to dismantling...

Dismantling The Traditional Narrative

If you had a broken bone or a high fever, you wouldn't be told to 'just get on with it'; you'd be offered care, rest and medical help. So, why should emotional pain be treated any differently? Depression, anxiety, trauma, burnout – these aren't just moods you can snap out of. They're real, valid experiences, and even if they can't be seen on the outside, they are just as valid as any physical pain.

Taking care of your mental health isn't a weakness. It's an act of self-respect. It's strength. Just like eating well, moving your body or going to the doctor when something feels off, tending to your emotional well-being is part of honouring yourself. It's vitally important that we gently challenge the belief that mental health struggles are made up or can simply be prayed away.

Destigmatising mental health

I want to gently encourage you to make space for mental health in your everyday language. Talk about how you're really feeling. Speak about your stress, your need for rest, your struggles. Let mental health become something normal, something that you and the people around you are allowed to prioritise without shame. 'The everyday mental health framework' exercise below provides a framework to get you started.

I also want to gently remind you that hiding your struggles doesn't make them go away. In fact, bottling them up only intensifies the pain. Imagine if you were carrying a heavy weight and refused to ask for help. Eventually, that weight would crush you. Seeking support isn't selfish or shameful; it's a way of lightening the load so you can move forward.

Exercise: The everyday mental health framework

Practise talking about your mental health in the same way you'd discuss your physical health. This structure shows you how to do that and suggests some example statements:

- **Use familiar comparisons**
    - **Example for physical health:** 'I pulled a muscle, so I need to rest today.'
    - **Mental health parallel:** 'I've been feeling emotionally drained, so I'm taking some time to recharge today.'
- **Emphasise self-care as maintenance**
    - **Example for physical health:** 'I go to the gym three times a week to stay fit.'
    - **Mental health parallel:** 'I meditate or go to the gym regularly to keep my mind healthy.'
- **Talk about seeking support**
    - **Example for physical health:** 'I saw a doctor because I've had a lingering cough.'
    - **Mental health parallel:** 'I'm working with a therapist to better manage my anxiety.'
- **Normalise fluctuations**
    - **Example for physical health:** 'I caught a cold, but I'm taking care of myself and resting.'

- **Mental health parallel:** 'I've been feeling low lately, but I'm focusing on things that help me feel better.'
- **Celebrate progress**
  - **Example for physical health:** 'I've been drinking more water and it's really helping my energy levels.'
  - **Mental health parallel:** 'I've been setting boundaries and it's making a big difference in how I feel.'
- **Acknowledge mental health in others**
  - **Example for physical health:** 'You've been working out – you look so energised!'
  - **Mental health parallel:** 'You've been practicing mindfulness – you seem so calm and grounded!'

Destigmatising mental health also means addressing the language we use. Words like *crazy, weak* or *attention-seeking* not only hurt but also perpetuate the stigma. Changing the way in which we talk about mental health can have a powerful ripple effect. When you speak openly about your emotions, when you name your struggles without shame, you create space for others to do the same. This isn't about forcing everyone around you to understand, though. It's about you creating a change in yourself first and working towards feeling heard and seen.

If you grew up in a household where mental health was never discussed, the idea of talking about it might feel strange or even terrifying. You may sit and think, *They won't understand anyway.* You might feel as though you're breaking a cultural rule – and in some ways, you are, but breaking that rule is necessary for change. By speaking up, you're not only advocating for yourself, you're saying, 'Whether you understand or not, I am still choosing to make space for it.'

Remember, the struggles you're facing are deeply rooted in the cultural context we've all grown up with. For many of you in the South Asian community, mental health was probably never truly talked about. There's a natural fear of the unknown, and mental health can feel like unfamiliar territory. Educating yourself and those around you about mental health is a powerful first step towards change, and by normalising mental health care, you're not just breaking cycles of shame; you're building a foundation of self-awareness, compassion and strength.

Marriage is not a cure-all

In the South Asian community, the assumption is that having a husband or starting a family will give you stability and purpose, wiping away any emotional pain, anxiety or depression. But the truth is, marriage is a partnership that requires emotional wellness and growth to thrive, and entering it with unresolved struggles can often amplify those challenges rather than easing them. What marriage isn't is a cure for mental health issues, so let's dismantle this myth together.

If you've ever struggled with your mental health, you know how deeply it can affect your day-to-day life. You may experience low energy, have difficulty trusting others or feel overwhelmed by emotions. If you carry unprocessed wounds from childhood, they can show up in your relationships, including in your marriage. So, instead of marriage being a magical solution, it can actually intensify the pressures, forcing two people to carry not just their individual challenges but the weight of the relationship, too. Here are some examples of the kinds of pressure you might experience when married:

- You're constantly expected to smooth over family conflicts or keep the peace at all costs.
- You're obliged to take on the role of caregiver in your home, perhaps both physically and emotionally, and can't consider your own needs.
- You're forced to suppress your own emotions and needs to meet the demands of your in-laws and keep the focus on their happiness.
- You've internalised the belief that your worth is measured by how well you 'hold everything together'.
- You feel that asking for help, especially mental health support, would be seen as weakness or failure.

None of this is to say marriage isn't valuable. It absolutely is, but it flourishes when both individuals are aware and understand themselves better, are emotionally ready to build a partnership and are not using marriage as an escape from their own pain.

As a therapist, let me remind you that no relationship, no matter how much love it holds, can replace the personal work that healing requires, and it's unfair to place that responsibility on your partner, expecting them to be your saviour. That kind of pressure will create an unsustainable strain on any relationship.

BUILDING A PARTNERSHIP

Instead of seeing marriage as the 'solution', let's reframe it as a partnership, a space where two people who've worked on themselves come together to grow. A healthy marriage is built on trust, communication and mutual respect.

You deserve to enter a marriage feeling resilient in yourself, knowing that you're not relying on your partner to 'fix' you. That doesn't mean you need to have everything figured out before getting married – nobody does – but it means taking steps towards understanding your own needs, emotions and patterns before you expect someone else to navigate them with you.

A flourishing marriage is one where both people support each other's growth, not one where one person is burdened with healing the other. When I say this, I hear things like, 'Well, isn't he supposed to be there for me?' and 'If I can't go to him, who am I meant to go to?' And I hear you. Both of you are needed by each other and need to be there for each other, yet one person cannot be everything for you. If you are unable to self-soothe – if you don't even know what needs soothing – you'll be unable to tell your husband how to support you, or even what it is you need support on.

I encourage you to at least start on that work prior to entering a marriage, so you have some clarity beforehand. This doesn't mean you won't continue learning and growing when you're married, but things like self-awareness, managing emotions in a healthy way, positive communication, boundaries, confidence and so on are things you can start working on now. The 'Dismantling the marriage myth' exercise below is a good starting point.

Exercise: Dismantling the marriage myth

This exercise is here to help you slow down and come back to yourself, before the noise, before the expectations, before the pressure to perform a role you might not feel ready for. Whether you're considering marriage, feeling pushed towards it or questioning your readiness, these reflections are a chance to tune into your emotional well-being and make choices from a place of clarity, not fear or guilt:

- **Ask yourself why you want marriage:** Reflect on your reasons for wanting to get married. Is it because you feel pressured by family or society? Is it because you believe it will fix something in your life? Write down your thoughts and notice if they're rooted in external expectations or internal readiness.
- **Focus on your emotional wellness first:** Work on building your emotional resilience before entering a partnership. Consider journalling, mindfulness practices or even therapy to explore unresolved pain, patterns or limiting beliefs. The more you understand yourself, the more likely you are to thrive in a relationship.
- **Set boundaries with cultural expectations:** If you're feeling pressured to marry because of cultural expectations, practice setting boundaries. This could mean calmly explaining to your family that you want to take time to focus on yourself first. Boundaries don't need to be harsh. They're about honouring your needs while remaining respectful.
- **Normalise seeking support:** It's okay to need help before or during a marriage, whether its pre-marital counselling or couples' therapy. Break the stigma around mental health by reminding yourself that seeking support is a strength, not a weakness.

The healthier you are as an individual, the stronger your relationships will be. By dismantling the narrative that marriage is a cure-all, you create space to approach marriage as a conscious choice rather than a cultural expectation.

Religion and therapy can coexist

Right, let's talk about this once and for all. Faith and religion hold immense significance in the lives of many South Asian families. For many, they're a source of strength, comfort and guidance during the most difficult times, yet when it comes to mental health, they're often wrongly invoked. For example, if you've been suffering emotional distress, you may have been told, 'This is a test from God – your faith isn't strong enough.' While these words probably come from a place of love and genuine belief, they can unintentionally invalidate the depth and complexity of mental health challenges, leaving those who are struggling feeling unsupported or misunderstood.

Let me assure you, though, that your faith and mental health can coexist in a beautiful, supportive way. They don't have to be separate, and they're definitely not at odds with each other. Faith can give you incredible hope, strength and resilience, but it doesn't have to carry the entire weight of your healing journey. When you embrace both your faith and your mental health together, you create space for a more compassionate, balanced approach. You don't have to choose one over the other. It's not about separating them but about seeing the bigger picture, where both can nurture you. For example:

- Feeling anxious or depressed doesn't mean your faith is lacking.
- Struggling with your mental health doesn't mean you've failed spiritually.
- Mental health challenges are simply part of being human, shaped by your biology, your experiences and life's ups and downs.
- You're not alone in struggling and there's no shame in reaching out for support.

I know it can be incredibly difficult when mental health struggles are misunderstood, especially within South Asian communities. I've seen situations where families might think their daughter hasn't married by a certain age because someone has given her the 'evil eye', or they might believe she's possessed rather than recognising the symptoms of a mental health issue like schizophrenia.

While seeking spiritual guidance can certainly offer comfort and peace, it's also important to recognise when professional mental health support is needed. A religious scholar or healer may provide relief, but they aren't trained to diagnose or treat mental health conditions. Understanding this distinction doesn't mean you're rejecting your faith; it's an act of deep care and respect for your well-being.

One thing I repeatedly say is that it's absolutely essential to have holistic, tailored support where you feel seen and heard, and where you can bring in your faith while also managing your mental health. You can have a spiritual leader as well as a mental health professional, and you can even find mental health professionals who create a faith-sensitive space for you.

Faith communities themselves can benefit from mental health education, learning that prayer or religious rituals can coexist with therapy, medication or other forms of support. For example, if you or someone you love is struggling with depression, praying for strength can provide spiritual reassurance and emotional regulation, but it's equally important to see a therapist who can help you explore and find ways to manage. The two approaches don't cancel each other out; they complement one another.

Educating families and communities about the difference between spiritual issues and mental health challenges can also help reduce shame. When we reframe mental health as a health issue, similar to a trapped nerve or diabetes, it becomes easier to talk about it and to seek help without feeling judged. In the same way you would see a doctor for a physical illness, you can see a therapist for emotional or mental struggles. Both approaches are acts of self-care, not signs of weakness. In no way does it mean you've given up on God or your faith is weak.

Try using the 'Faith and feelings journal' exercise below to help you navigate the intersection of religion and mental health.

Exercise: Faith and feelings journal

This exercise will help you clarify your thoughts and affirm that your faith and mental health can work hand in hand:

- **Create a safe space for reflection:** Find a quiet moment to reflect on your struggles in the context of your faith. Open a journal and write about how your beliefs support you and where you feel tension between your mental health needs and religious expectations.
- **Write down affirmations:** Consider affirmations that integrate your faith with mental health. For example, 'God wants me to seek help when I'm struggling because my well-being matters' or 'I can be a person of faith while also receiving therapy.'
- **Identify resources:** Write down trusted resources that support both your faith and your mental health. These could include compassionate religious scholars who understand mental health, therapists who respect your faith or supportive friends and family.
- **Plan your next steps:** If you're struggling, list practical actions that blend faith and mental health support. For example, you might include a daily prayer or recitation, scheduling a therapy session or having an open conversation with a loved one about your feelings.

A message that I really want you to absorb when I speak about religion and mental health, regardless of the religion you're from, is that, just like your body, your mind is there to be looked after – and wouldn't God want you to look after it? Faith is a powerful anchor and, as a therapist, I have heard first-hand testimony from many people who say faith is very protective – but so is the strength it takes to seek help when needed. You deserve both.

The perfection illusion

You may feel the weight of expectations everywhere you look. Whether it's your family comparing you to a cousin who's more successful, social media highlighting someone's perfect life or even cultural narratives praising women who have it all, the pressure can feel debilitating. Comparison culture is a deeply engrained habit in many of our communities, passed down through generations and reinforced by well-meaning but harmful comments like, 'Look how well she's doing. Why can't you do the same?'

In the age of social media, these comparisons have only intensified. You might find yourself scrolling through photos of people who seem to have the perfect job, the ideal relationship or the dream body and wondering, *Why isn't my life like that?* But the truth is, what you see online is rarely the full picture. Social media offers a highlights reel, not the behind-the-scenes reality. The polished images and celebratory posts don't capture the struggles, insecurities or challenges that every person inevitably faces, so when we compare ourselves to these carefully curated moments, we measure our lives against an unrealistic standard. Comparison culture can weigh heavily on how you view your worth, especially within our communities. There's often a hierarchy based on things like education, career success, marriage or motherhood. If you feel like you're not meeting these markers or not meeting them fast enough, it's easy to spiral into feelings of inadequacy. I know it can be hard not to compare when you notice what you don't have and what you want. It can feel overwhelming at times. But your path is your own, and I want you to remember the following key points:

- **Your worth is not a checklist:** It's not based on meeting societal or community standards of success.
- **Your journey is uniquely yours:** You don't have to follow anyone else's timeline.

- **You are valuable just as you are:** That's regardless of where you are in your personal journey.
- **Sometimes, we forget to appreciate what we do have:** So, make a point of reminding yourself.
- **What you have may be something others yearn for:** This is exactly the same as you yearning for what they have.
- **Comparison can rob you of peace:** However, gratitude for what you've achieved at your own pace can help you reconnect with your own strength.

SOCIAL MEDIA IN THE BALANCE

Social media and cultural norms can certainly fuel comparison, and they may be a source of great pain, but they can also be powerful tools for empowerment and support. I know that social media has become a community for many of you, and platforms like Instagram or TikTok can offer education, inspiration and connection when used thoughtfully. They have the potential to introduce you to groups of women who are challenging the very stereotypes you've been burdened with, or to therapists and activists who offer practical advice for self-growth. But balance is crucial. If scrolling through your feed leaves you feeling drained, inadequate or less than, it's time to step back and reassess how you engage with these platforms.

I know many of you may have found me through social media, and perhaps my words or my page have been a source of connection and comfort. That's wonderful. But remember: if it's not serving you any more, it's okay to hit reset. Here's what I want you to keep in mind:

- **Social media can uplift and empower:** But only if you use it to connect with supportive, like-minded communities.
- **It's a place to discover resources:** Whether it's for self-growth, learning or inspiration, there's so much there.
- **Balance is key:** If scrolling is leaving you feeling worse about yourself, it's time to step back and reflect on what you're consuming.
- **Declutter your feed:** If what you see no longer serves you, unfollow accounts that make you feel inadequate and curate a feed that nourishes you.
- **You have the power to choose:** It's okay to take breaks and reset as and when you need to.

Instead of focusing on what others have that you don't, focus on your unique strengths, values and journey. Remind yourself that no one else has lived your life or faced your challenges, and that's what makes your path so uniquely yours. Be realistic in your expectations, not just of yourself but also of others. No one has it all figured out, and even those who seem the most put together often carry unseen struggles, yet we don't pay attention to that: our mind goes straight to living through these picture-perfect posts and reels.

Remember also that it's okay to grow, to want more and to build things for yourself while also reminding yourself of the things that once made you happy. Sometimes, you may have been doing well, but then the things that used to make you happy stopped doing so because you started focusing on the lives of others on social media. The 'Personal growth versus comparison' exercise below will help you take a step back and ensure you're focusing on what's important: you.

Exercise: Personal growth versus comparison

Create a simple chart that visually emphasises your personal growth instead of comparison. The purpose is to shift the focus from others to yourself and remind yourself that everyone's journey is unique.

Take a sheet of paper and divide it into two columns, one titled 'Their path' (which is the external comparisons you make) and the other 'My path' (which is your personal focus). In the 'Their path' column, list the points of comparison you find yourself using, such as career success, relationships or physical appearance. In the 'My path' column, write your own goals or values related to those areas. For example:

Their path	My path
They bought a new house.	I'm saving for a cosy rental that feels right for me.
They look flawless on social media.	I'm focusing on feeling healthy and confident in my skin.

Embracing your roots

As you navigate healing, remember that reconnecting with the richness of your culture can be a powerful source of pride and grounding. You don't have to choose between who you are and who you're becoming.

The beauty of your roots is always there, offering strength as you move forwards. Take your time, and know that you're not alone in this process.

One of the most beautiful aspects of South Asian culture is the deep sense of community. I want you to think about all the things you love. From shared meals around a family table to joyous festivals that bring neighbourhoods alive, there's a collective spirit that encourages connection and belonging.

The value placed on relationships, whether with family, friends or even neighbours, can be a source of strength during life's hardest moments. You're never truly alone. There's always someone to check in on you, offer a cup of tea or simply sit with you in silence. This interconnectedness, when nurtured, can create an invaluable sense of safety and support.

The colourful lights, the vibrant clothing, the mouthwatering food and the music fill the senses with life. These moments remind us of the beauty of tradition and the importance of pausing to celebrate, no matter what life brings. South Asian culture is filled with creativity, including art forms that have stood the test of time. From the intricate designs of henna to the vibrant patterns of sarees, salwar kameez and lehengas, there's artistry in even the smallest details. This creativity is such an amazing way to find joy, grounding, mindfulness or a hobby to improve your well-being.

There's also an inherent resilience in the culture, passed down through generations. Our ancestors faced the immense challenges of colonialism, migration and displacement, yet they thrived and built lives filled with meaning and beauty. This resilience is part of your inheritance, too, showing you that we're capable of navigating adversity with strength and grace.

Adaptability is another symbol of our culture. Whether it's creating recipes, embracing new languages or finding ways to honour traditions while living in a different country, South Asians have mastered the art of blending the old with the new. There's a reason our homes are known for their warmth. Guests are treated like family, often greeted with elaborate meals, endless cups of chai and heartfelt conversations. This culture of generosity reflects the belief that joy multiplies when shared.

Reconnecting with this hospitality, whether as a host or a guest, can reignite a sense of purpose and belonging. It's not just about giving; it's about creating spaces of love and care that remind us of our shared humanity and values like respect for elders, humility, gratitude and duty to others. While these values can sometimes feel overwhelming when imposed, they also carry profound nourishment for the soul when embraced with balance.

As you navigate your personal journey, take a moment to pause and reflect on the beauty within your culture. The stories that shaped your childhood and the strength of that community are not just pieces of your heritage; they are pieces of you.

By embracing the beauty of your roots, you reclaim the parts of your identity that bring joy and meaning. You recreate what culture means for you. You don't have to choose between your culture and your individuality; you can honour both. Let your culture be a source of pride and inspiration. It holds the power to ground you, connect you and remind you of the beauty of being exactly who you are. The 'Cultural mood board challenge' exercise below provides a structured way for you to explore what your heritage means to you.

Exercise: Cultural mood board challenge

Let's be creative and create a vibrant cultural mood board to visually reconnect with your heritage!

1. **Gather inspiration:** Look for photos of traditional outfits, food, festivals, art or family moments. Include cultural symbols, colours and quotes that resonate with you.
2. **Create your board:** Use a physical corkboard or an app like Pinterest or Canva. Arrange your items creatively – think fabrics, patterns and textures that remind you of home.
3. **Add a personal touch:** Write a short caption for each item, sharing why it matters to you or a memory tied to it.
4. **Display it proudly:** Place your mood board somewhere visible to remind yourself of your roots daily – and don't forget to have fun with it!

Thriving through therapy

For many of you, life is about juggling responsibilities and meeting expectations. You're raised with the idea that being selfless is a virtue and that focusing on yourself is selfish (*see* box on the next page). Therapy challenges that narrative by saying you can only pour from a cup that isn't empty. Seeking professional help is a way to refill your cup, to build yourself up so you can continue to show up for those you care about. Therapy doesn't mean forgetting or abandoning your cultural values; it means finding a way to thrive within them. It's about aligning your mental health with your spiritual, cultural and personal beliefs.

Consider how therapy can work alongside your values and who you are. A therapist can help you explore your emotions and experiences while respecting your cultural values, religious beliefs, and family dynamics. For example, they may help you process feelings of guilt or shame in a way that honours your cultural and spiritual identity rather than dismissing it. Therapy gives you the tools to approach life's challenges with clarity and resilience while staying grounded in who you are.

When we reframe therapy as an act of self-love, it stops being something to hide or feel ashamed about. Instead, it becomes a gift you give yourself – a step towards healing and growing. You're not weak for seeking help. You're strong for recognising that you don't have to do it all alone.

Selfish or honouring yourself?

I know that seeking professional help for your mental health can feel overwhelming, especially when it's not something that your parents, elders or community are familiar with. It's natural for them to feel uncertain or even intimidated by the idea. Sometimes, it may even feel like they're attempting to silence or shame you by calling you selfish for wanting to prioritise your own needs. I often hear how the younger generation is seen as 'selfish', as though focusing on yourself is wrong. But it's important to see this in a different light.

For so long, your life may have been centred on others – living for them, caring for them – but now, as more resources become available and more people are reaching out for help, it's okay to create some space for *you*. Here's what I want you to understand:

- **Taking care of yourself doesn't mean you're abandoning others:** It means you're learning how to nurture yourself so you can show up for those you love in a healthier way.
- **You deserve to heal at your own pace:** That doesn't mean letting go of everything that matters to you, whether it's your culture, faith or loved ones. Those things are still part of you.

→

- **Being 'selfish' can actually help you be more selfless:** When you take the time to focus on your own growth, you're strengthening yourself for the relationships and communities you care about.
- **Healing doesn't erase your roots:** It's a journey of learning to be an individual while still honouring your sense of togetherness and community.

CULTURALLY SENSITIVE THERAPISTS

For therapy to truly serve the South Asian community, it must reflect the unique cultural and social dynamics of our lives. Many therapists, even with the best intentions, may overlook how deeply engrained concepts like family honour, respect for elders or religious devotion shape our experiences. Without this understanding, therapy can feel alienating – as if it's asking you to shed a part of yourself to fit into a different mould. But therapy doesn't have to be that way.

Imagine sitting with a therapist who truly understands why your family's opinion matters so much to you, or why honour and shame aren't just individual concepts but linked to your family's identity. Imagine feeling seen, not judged, when you explain how your role as a daughter, sister or wife impacts your mental health. When therapists take the time to understand these nuances, therapy becomes a safe and empowering space where you can explore your struggles without feeling like you're betraying your roots.

Cultural sensitivity in therapy also means recognising the importance of religious and spiritual values. For many in the South Asian community, faith isn't just a belief system; it's a way of life. A therapist who respects this can help you use your faith as a source of strength rather than seeing it as an obstacle. For instance, they might explore how your religious teachings encourage forgiveness, boundaries, compassion or patience, helping you integrate these values into your healing journey – or how it teaches what love looks like, what connections give you and what community means.

Family dynamics are another crucial area. In South Asian families, boundaries often blur and individual decisions can ripple across the entire family. A culturally sensitive therapist understands that setting boundaries isn't about shutting people out but rather finding a balance that respects both your needs and your family's role in your life.

When therapists approach their work with cultural humility and sensitivity, they create a bridge between mental health treatment and the rich, complex realities of South Asian life. This bridge is essential, not only for encouraging more women to seek help but also for ensuring that therapy feels relevant, respectful and transformative.

The exercise below will help you find a culturally sensitive therapist who meets your needs.

Exercise: Finding a culturally and/or faith-sensitive therapist

This exercise is about identifying a therapist who's the right fit for you. It will empower you to evaluate therapists to ensure they understand and respect your cultural and spiritual background while providing effective care. It is crucial to find an accredited therapist who belongs to the right organisations. See p. 218 for more information.

1. **Reflect on your needs**
   - Before meeting a therapist, spend a few moments thinking about what you need:
     - What role do your culture and faith play in your identity and values?
     - Are there specific struggles tied to your cultural or spiritual background you want to address?
     - Do you want your therapist to incorporate faith-based practices or maintain a neutral perspective while respecting your beliefs?

2. **Questions to ask during a consultation**
   - How do you incorporate cultural sensitivity in your practice? (Look for openness to learning about your background and experience of working with diverse clients.)
   - Have you worked with clients from South Asian backgrounds or similar cultural contexts before? (It's not mandatory for the therapist to share your background, but experience matters.)
   - How do you balance understanding cultural traditions with addressing individual needs? (Assess if they respect cultural nuances without letting them overshadow your individuality.)

- Are you comfortable discussing faith and spirituality in therapy? (If faith is central to your life, it's important that your therapist values this part of your identity.)
- How do you incorporate (or accommodate) a client's faith into therapeutic work? (If this is important to you, listen for ways in which they support integrating faith-based practices such as prayer and reflection on scripture.)
- What's your perspective on the relationship between faith and mental health? (A therapist who's a good fit will acknowledge that faith can be a source of strength and healing, while also respecting mental health as a valid area for support.)
- What's your approach to therapy and how do you adapt it to different cultural or spiritual contexts? (Ensure their methods – cognitive behavioural therapy, humanistic, mindfulness and so on – feel compatible with your values and needs.)
- How do you handle conflicts between cultural expectations and a client's personal goals? (Look for strategies that help you navigate cultural pressures without dismissing their significance.)
- How do you ensure a safe, non-judgemental space for clients? (This gives you a sense of how they create emotional safety, especially around topics like family dynamics, identity or stigma.)
- How do you handle confidentiality, especially in culturally close-knit communities? (Assurance about privacy is vital if you're worried about judgement or gossip.)

3. **Pay attention to these things**
    - During the conversation, be cautious if the therapist does any of the following:
        - Makes generalised statements about your culture or faith (for example, brings up stereotypes)
        - Dismisses the importance of your cultural or spiritual values
        - Avoids answering questions about cultural or faith sensitivity
        - Seems uncomfortable discussing topics related to your identity

Remember, the right therapist will not simply see your culture and faith as parts of your identity; they will honour them as strengths and integrate them into your healing journey.

Conclusion

Congratulations! You've made it to the end of this book. Take a deep breath, and know that I'm so proud of you. Truly. Happy dance here!

Reading these words, letting them touch the parts of you that have long been hidden or silenced, is no small thing. You've done something powerful. You've chosen to face the truths many of us were taught to avoid. You've dared to ask questions of a culture that often demands obedience. And, most of all, you've made space for *yourself*. For every part of you: your voice, your needs, your pain, and your healing.

This book was never meant to have all the answers. Instead, it's about lighting a small lamp in the dark, offering you language, validation and a sense of being *seen* as you walk a path that was never clearly laid out for you. You don't need to have it all figured out. You don't need to be perfectly healed or completely free from the weight you carry. What matters is that you start telling the truth to yourself, start putting gentle boundaries in place, start choosing your peace over performance. Start being present. This is not the end of your story; this is the beginning of your becoming.

You're allowed to want more for yourself: more gentleness, more joy, more depth. You're allowed to ask yourself, *Who am I?* You're allowed to step out of the roles that never fit you and grow into a version of yourself that feels whole. And if ever you doubt your worth, I want you to remember: you are not here to carry everyone else's expectations. You are here to live. To embrace each part of what makes you *you* – including your culture.

Take what you've learned, hold it close and let it shape the next chapter of your life: one that is rooted not in fear but in freedom.

I'm walking alongside you. You've got this.

Resources

Useful tools

WEBSITES

The Centre for Clinical Interventions (Australia)
cci.health.wa.gov.au

Think CBT
thinkcbt.com/think-cbt-worksheets

APPS
Calm
Calm Harm
MindShift CBT
My Possible Self
What's Up?

BOOKS

Bhattacharya, Piyali, *Good Girls Marry Doctors: South Asian American Daughters on Obedience and Rebellion* (Aunt Lute Books, 2016)

Chatterjee, Rangan, *Make Change That Lasts* (Penguin Life, 2023)

Durvasula, Ramani, *It's Not You: Identifying and Healing from Narcissistic Relationships* (BenBella Books, 2024)

Tsabary, Shefali, *The Parenting Map: Step-by-Step Solutions to Consciously Create the Ultimate Parent-Child Relationship* (Atria Books, 2023)

PODCASTS

Brown Girl Self-Care by Bre Mitchell
podcasts.apple.com/us/podcast/brown-girl-self-care/id1463356560

That Desi Spark
instagram.com/thatdesispark

The Self Love Fix by Beatrice Kamau
podcasts.apple.com/us/podcast/the-self-love-fix/id1449341581

VIDEOS

Brown Girls Living Alone Part 2
tiktok.com/@fahima.therapy/video/7215275069092678918

How to access therapy

Counselling Directory
counselling-directory.org.uk

Muslim Counsellor & Psychotherapist Network
mcapn.co.uk/counselling-directory

Peace by Piece
peacebypiece.co

Psychology Today
psychologytoday.com

The Black, African and Asian Therapy Network
baatn.org.uk

An invitation

We've walked through some tender, difficult truths together. As Brown women, so many of us have carried pain quietly, sometimes for years. Revisiting these wounds, even through the safety of words, can stir up emotions that feel overwhelming. If you've made it this far, I want to say: *you are deeply courageous*. This work isn't easy. And you've done it.

And I don't want you to do the rest alone.

If this book has resonated with you, I warmly invite you to join our growing community because healing feels softer when we do it together.

Join 'Threads That Hold Us' on Discord (discord.com/invite/Meg794PHk)
This is a gentle online space I've created for women who are exploring identity, healing, emotional safety, and most importantly, working on learning how to come back to yourself. It's a place for reflection, connection and support; a space to be held and to hold others, without judgement.

Follow along on TikTok and Instagram
Find me at **@fahima.therapy**, where I share thoughtful reminders, videos and healing prompts to support your journey. Whether you're in the thick of your healing or just beginning, I'll be there with you.

Be part of our Common-unity
You belong here. Your story matters. And in this shared space, we rebuild together.

Let's put ourselves back together, **peace by piece**.

Acknowledgements

To my parents, thank you for your presence, your support and everything you've taught me along the way. This book exists because of the experiences we've shared and the tough truths we've lived through. My siblings, thank you for being a backbone during one of the most difficult times in my life. Even though you drive me mad half the time, somehow we always find our way back to each other through laughter. Our bond holds more strength than we often say out loud.

A special acknowledgement to my little sister, Hafiza. I'm so proud of the woman you're becoming and so excited to witness your journey into becoming a therapist.

To my friends, thank you for being there through the hardest parts of this journey. You sat with me through the tears, reminded me to rest, encouraged me to keep going and held me when I felt overwhelmed. Your emotional support meant more than I can put into words.

To my clients, thank you for trusting me with your stories, your pain and your healing. You have taught me so much about resilience, hope and the strength it takes to face what hurts. Your journeys have deeply informed the pages of this book, and it's an honour to witness your growth. This book is a reflection of what I've learned from you.

To my online community, thank you for showing up and for sharing your own stories with me. You've been part of this process in ways you may not even realise. Your messages, your encouragement and your trust have helped me to continue writing and to realise that this book needed to exist.

To myself, thank you for staying with it. For writing through fear and doubt. For being honest even when it felt uncomfortable. For continuing to believe that healing is possible. You really did the thing. I'm proud of you.

This book is for all of us who are learning to understand ourselves more deeply. We are putting ourselves back together **peace by piece**.

Index

abusive relationships 54, 61, 63–5
accountability with empathy, generational trauma and 156–8
adaptability, South Asian 210
addictions 61
affection, lack of 61–2
affirmations, positive 94–5, 206
anxiety 42, 58, 62
apologies 149, 183
authentic living (being your full self) 158–78
author's story 10–15

beauty standards 98, 126–8
blame 141, 152–6, 170–1, 172, 183–4
bodily autonomy 135–6
boundaries 51, 59, 77–9, 102–3, 129–30, 149–50
    communicating your boundaries to your parents 167–71, 175
    setting gentle 130, 164–71

'caretaker' role 66
case studies
    Aaliya opens up to mother 196
    Alina and financial family responsibilities 150–1
    Amira opens up to her father 177–8
    Ayesha and the impact of sexual abuse 64
    Ayesha's constant availability 47–8
    Ayesha's journey to therapy 192–3
    Jarin's stolen life 70
    Jasmine's journey to rebuilding relationships 182
    Leena learns to move past blame 153–4
    marriage related
        Khadija's family ignore what she wants 132
        Salma and skin colour 127–8
        Yusra sees marriage as her only escape 132–3
    Maya: freedom from abusive relationship 54
    Nadia's loneliness, loss and depression 36–7
    Noor's shift to living consciously 53
    Priya and the loss of her sister to suicide 198–9
    Sameera's sacrifice and suppression 41–2
    Sana explores the impact of her tension-filled childhood home 72–3
celebrating your culture 78, 209–11
change, fear of 169–70
child abuse 12
clothing and traditional fashion 57, 210
communicating effectively 167–71, 172–6
community and cultural connections 74–5, 79–80, 209–11

comparison culture 193–4, 207–10
complex post-traumatic stress disorder (CPTSD) 11
conflict, handling 147–9
    blame and moving past it 152–6
    constructive conversations with your parents 167–78
    forgiveness 180–2
    where to draw the line 149–50
    see also boundaries
connection, importance of 10, 68–71
controlling behaviour 21–2, 57–8, 144–7

depersonalisation 10–11
depression *see* mental health
derealisation 10
divorce
    author's 13
    failure and judgement 109–12, 137–9
    handling 137–9
    rates 109
    reframing exercise 139
    shame and honour cycle 138–9
dysfunction, family 60–5

elders, healthy respect for 123–4, 128
    see also controlling behaviour; generational trauma
emotional independence 183
emotional suppression 24, 31, 41–2, 59
empathy and accountability, generational trauma and 156–8
endurance as strength, perception of 23–4
enmeshment 56–7, 74
    balance and boundaries 77–8
    community and cultural connections 74–5, 79–80
    healthy 75–6, 77–8
    letting go of 'What will people say?' 80–2
exercises
    10 small shifts 46–7
    balance and boundaries 77–9
    the balance tool 163–4
    blame-to-boundary transition 170–1
    community and cultural connections 74–5, 79–80
    create your real audience and find your voice 81–2
    cultural mood board challenge 211
    dismantling the marriage myth 203–4
    embrace both/and 162
    everyday mental health framework 200–1

faith and feelings journal 206
the family tree of patterns 157-8
finding a culturally and/or faith-sensitive therapist 213-15
friendship checklist 84-5
generational healing letter 44-5
healthy and unhealthy guilt 34-6
identifying friendship patterns 86-7
inheritance reflection 28-9
inner child healing box 171-2
on marriage: pausing for reflection 134
personal growth vs comparison 209
practise gentle boundaries 130
recognise your full self 162
recognising your triggers 176
redefining forgiveness for yourself 181-2
reflecting on how you feel about therapy 92-3
reflection and connection 159-61
reflections on a healthy relationship 119
reflections on beauty 127
reflections on being the perfect bride 125-6
reflections on friends and family 88-9
reframing divorce 139
self-limiting beliefs 31-2
support circle 164-6
translate your truth with care 173-4
two circles 30
values exploration 38-9
visibility practice 40-1
write your own life guide 49-51
external validation and healing 182-3

faith, religious 190-3, 204-7
family roles, rigid 65-6
finances/money 31, 106-7, 150-1
forgiveness 180-2
friendships 82-3, 88-90
    checklist 84-5
    identifying patterns 86-7
    parental suspicion of 67-71, 83
    recognising unhealthy 85-6

generational resilience 178-80
generational trauma 141-4, 183-4
    accountability with empathy 156-8
guilt and shame 28, 30, 33-6, 58, 80-1, 134, 135-6, 138-9, 146-7

'hero' role 66
hierarchy, family see authentic living (being your real self); boundaries; invisible life guide, South Asian; marriage; parents, constructive conversations with your; respect for elders, healthy

in-laws 102-5, 128-30
intentionally, living 52-3
intimacy, sexual 108-9, 135-6
invisible life guide, South Asian 20-1
    confronting and dismantling 26-54, 73-95, 112-40, 155-84, 199-
    controlling behaviour 21-2
    discovering your own journey 37-8
    failure to follow 25-6
    finding your voice 39
    guilt 33-6
    maternal role models 22-3, 28-9, 43-5
    the next generation 29
    self-doubt and self-limitation 29-32
    strength as an endurance test 23-4
    writing your own life guide 49-51
    see also authentic living (being your full self); boundaries; conflict, handling; controlling behaviour; exercises; marriage; mental health
isolation/disconnection 10-11, 59, 61-2, 66, 69-71

listening, active 90
loneliness 10-11, 59, 66
'lost child' role 66

marriage 21, 25, 53, 62
    abusive relationships 54
    arranged vs forced/coerced 96, 112-15
    building a partnership 203
    dismantling the traditional narrative 112-40
    handling proposals 101-2, 115
    healthy relationships 115-20
    in-laws 102-5, 128-30
    mature love 120
    menstruation and intimacy 107-9, 135-6
    pause, assess, proceed framework 114
    perfect bride narrative 124-6
    'protection' as control 105-7
    saying 'no' 115
    traditional narrative 96-7, 124-5
    as the 'ultimate fix' 188-90, 202-4
    weddings 121-4
    worthiness 97-100, 124-6
    see also divorce; maternal role models
'mascot' role 66
maternal role models 22-3, 28-9, 43-5, 86-7, 150
mature love 120
menstruation 107-8, 136
mental health 36-7, 42, 58, 62, 185-6
    being sent away 190
    challenges of second-generation children 194-5
    comparison culture 193-4, 207-10
    embracing your roots 209-11
    marriage as the 'ultimate fix' 188-90, 202-4
    religious faith 190-3, 204-7
    suicide and self-harm 198-9
    therapy taboo 196-7
    the traditional narrative 186-97
        dismantling 199-215
    see also therapy

opinions/judgement, other people's 57-60, 109-12, 137-9, 182-3, 193-4

parents, constructive conversations with your 167-71, 172-6
parents' relationships, our 21, 62, 72-3, 133, 150-1
people pleasing 59
perfectionism, toxic 62
physical appearance 98, 126-8
privacy, therapy and family 71-3
proposals, marriage 101-2, 115
protection narrative, women's need for 105-7

rebellion see authentic living (being your full self)
reconciliation/rebuilding relationships 181, 182
relationships/marriages, healthy 115-20
religious faith 190-3, 204-7
resilience, generational 178-80, 210
respect for elders, healthy 123-4, 128
    see also controlling behaviour; generational trauma
roots, embracing your 78, 209-11
rules, unspoken see invisible life guide, South Asian

sacrifice, self- 41-2
    see also maternal role models
safe-spaces, community 74-5, 80
scapegoating 65
second-generation children, challenges of 194-5
secrets/dysfunction, family 60-5
self-compassion 81, 94-5
self-doubt 29-30, 59, 62
self-harm and suicide 198-9
self-limiting beliefs 31-2
sexual abuse 12, 64
sexual intimacy and desire 108-9, 135-6
shame see guilt and shame
sibling dynamics 145-6

skin colour 98, 127–8
social media 207–9
suicide and self-harm 198–9
support, importance of 13–14, 69–72, 82–3, 164–6, 210

therapy
    and cultural sensitivity 91–2, 213–15
    and family privacy 71–3
    as a healing tool 93–4, 211–13
    myths and taboos 93, 196–7
    preparing for 92–5
    and religious faith 204–6
time for yourself, making 47–8
traditional narratives
    see authentic living (being your real self); divorce;
            invisible life guide, traditional South Asian;
            marriage; mental health

values, exploring your 38–9
voice, finding your 39–41, 57–8

weddings 102, 121–4